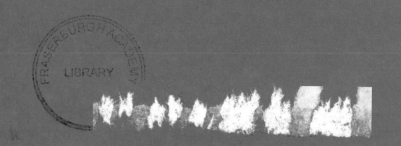

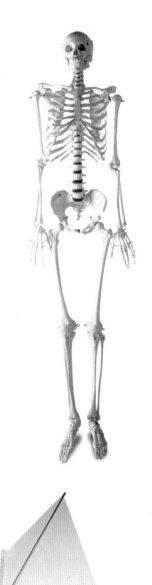

DK Children's Picture Encyclopedia

Claire Llewellyn

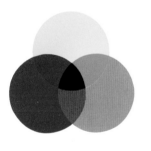

DORLING KINDERSLEY
London • New York • Stuttgart • Moscow

A DORLING KINDERSLEY BOOK

Project Editor Carey Combe
Art Editor Marcus James

Editors Patricia Grogan, Katherine Moss
Designers Sarah Cowley, Jacqueline Gooden, Joanna Hinton-Malivoire, Dean Price

DTP Designer Almudena Díaz

Managing Editor Jane Yorke
Managing Art Editor Chris Scollen

Picture Research James Clarke, Sally Hamilton
Picture Research Manager Melissa Albany

Production Josie Alabaster

Illustrators David Ashby, Chris Horsey, Janos Maffy

Consultants
Sally Whitton, Educational Consultant
Richard Woff, British Museum Education Service
Dale Buckton, DK Cartography

First published in Great Britain in 1997 by
Dorling Kindersley Limited
9 Henrietta Street, London WC2E 8PS

Visit us on the World Wide Web at
http://www.dk.com

A CIP catalogue record for this book is available
from the British Library.

ISBN 0-7513-5491-0

Colour reproducion by Colourscan, Singapore
Printed and bound in Italy by Mondadori

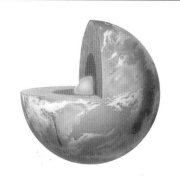

Contents

About this book
4

A to Z entry pages

Africa to Weather
6

World map
148

World map: continents
150

United Kingdom
151

World history timeline
152

Index
154

Acknowledgments
159

About this book

It's easy to find what you're looking for in **The DK Children's Picture Encyclopedia**. The large headings of each main entry tell you what each page is about. These are arranged alphabetically to help you quickly look up subjects that interest you.

Main entries
There are 145 exciting main entries to look up and learn about.

Alphabet
Use the alphabet at the top of the page to help you find your place in the encyclopedia.

Index
If you can't find the topic you are looking for, it may not be a main subject. Look it up in the index to find out which page it is on.

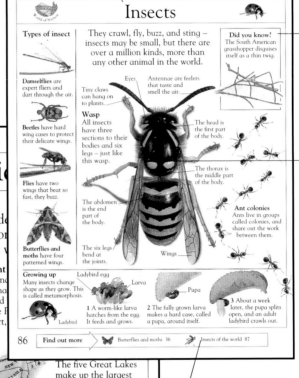

A B C D E F G H **I** J K L M N O P Q R S T U V W X Y Z

Insects

They crawl, fly, buzz, and sting – insects may be small, but there are over a million kinds, more than any other animal in the world.

Types of insect

Damselflies are expert fliers and dart through the air.

Beetles have hard wing cases to protect their delicate wings.

Flies have two wings that beat so fast, they buzz.

Butterflies and moths have four patterned wings.

Eyes
Antennae are feelers that taste and smell the air.

Tiny claws can hang on to plants.

Wasp
All insects have three sections to their bodies and six legs – just like this wasp.

The head is the first part of the body.

The thorax is the middle part of the body.

The abdomen is the end part of the body.

The six legs bend at the joints.

Wings

Did you know?
The South American grasshopper disguises itself as a thin twig.

Ant colonies
Ants live in groups called colonies, and share out the work between them.

Growing up
Many insects change shape as they grow. This is called metamorphosis.

Ladybird egg
Larva
Pupa

1 A worm-like larva hatches from the egg. It feeds and grows.

Ladybird

2 The fully grown larva makes a hard case, called a pupa, around itself.

3 About a week later, the pupa splits open, and an adult ladybird crawls out.

86 Find out more   Butterflies and moths 36   Insects of the world 87

"Did you know?"
Every page has a "Did you know?" box with a fascinating fact about the subject for you to discover.

Exciting photographs
Each page is full of colourful close-up photographs, and many feature step-by-step sequences.

A B C D E F G H I J K L M **N** O P Q

North Ameri[ca]

USA and Mexico
With mountains in the north and de[serts] in the south, North America has so[me of] the most spectacular scenery in the w[orld.]

Rocky Mountains
The Rockies stretch for 4,800 km (3,000 miles) down the western side of the USA.

Monument [Valley]
These san[d] rocks ha[ve been] carved [...] in the [...] Desert, [...]

The five Great Lakes make up the largest area of fresh water in the world.

Everglades
This vast tropical marsh in Florida is home to animals such as alligators.

Collared lizard
This lizard manages to survive in the dry deserts.

Grand Canyon
This deep, rocky gorge has been cut out in Arizona by the River Colorado.

Death Valley
Death Valley in California is the hottest, driest place in the whole of North America.

Sonoran Desert
This desert lies between the USA and Mexico. It is famous for its giant cacti.

Okefenokee swamp
This freshwater swamp in southern Georgia is a safe refuge for wildlife.

104 Find out more   Desert animals 45   Water 146

Picture cross-references
At the bottom of each page, you will find out where to look for more information on related subjects.

Illustrated maps
Large picture maps on many pages help you learn about different parts of the world.

Sub-entries
Every page has lots of sub-entries giving you more information about the main subject. You can find these by using the index.

4

Find out more

Each main entry belongs in one of five key subject areas, indicated by the symbol in the top left-hand corner of the page. The picture cross-references at the bottom of the page offer suggestions for other entries to look up.

Life in the Past
Learn all about ancient civilizations and prehistoric life in this key subject area.

World of Nature
This subject area covers the natural world from birds to polar lands.

Continents of the World
Information about regions, countries, and continents is found in this key subject area.

Polar lands

The polar lands lie around the north and south poles. The frozen ground and icy climate make them a hard place for plants to grow.

Icefield
A lot of the land in the polar regions is covered in huge areas of ice, called icefields.

Glaciers flow from the icefields.

Glaciers are rivers of ice that move slowly down mountain slopes.

Antarctica
No-one lives in the Antarctic, but scientists visit to study the land and its wildlife.

Tundra
The tundra is the frozen

Polar plants

Mosses grow in thick cushions. This protects them from icy winds.

The **Arctic wormwood** stores food in its roots to help it survive.

Grasses grow quickly in the spring when there are long periods of daylight.

Primroses have long roots to help them survive.

Life in the Arctic
People have lived in the Arctic for thousands of years. They have had to adapt their lifestyle to the harsh climate.

Winter coat

Dog-pulled sleds make it possible to move goods across the ice.

Warm clothes are made from animal skins.

Sled

Husky dog

Fleabane grows only for a few weeks in the Arctic summer.

Antarctica 19   Polar animals 111

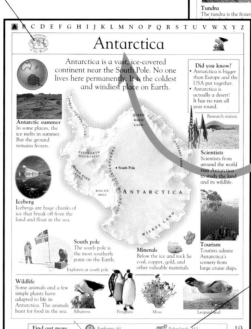

Antarctica

Antarctica is a vast, ice-covered continent near the South Pole. No one lives here permanently. It is the coldest and windiest place on Earth.

Did you know?
• Antarctica is bigger than Europe and the USA put together.
• Antarctica is actually a desert! It has no rain all year round.

Antarctic summer
In some places, the ice melts in summer. But the ground remains frozen.

Research station

Iceberg
Icebergs are huge chunks of ice that break off from the land and float in the sea.

Scientists
Scientists from around the world visit Antarctica to study the land and its wildlife.

South pole
The south pole is the most southerly point on the Earth.

Explorers at south pole

Minerals
Below the ice and rock lie coal, copper, gold, and other valuable materials.

Tourism
Tourists admire Antarctica's scenery from large cruise ships.

Wildlife
Some animals and a few simple plants have adapted to life in Antarctica. The animals hunt for food in the sea.

Albatross   Penguins   Moss   Leopard seal

Find out more   Explorers 61   Polar lands 112   19

The picture cross-references guide you to other main entries.

Life Today
If you look up topics in this key subject area, you will find out about everything from transport to sport.

Explorers

Travellers

Pacific Islanders were the first to cross the Pacific Ocean.

The Vikings sailed to the south to find fertile farmland.
Viking helmet

Merchants explored the route between China and Europe to trade in silk.

Arabs travelled in the 13th century to trade and find new lands.

Columbus, a Spanish explorer, crossed the Atlantic Ocean using an astrolabe.
Astrolabe

For thousands of years people have explored the world, hoping to find fertile farmland, fine goods, and riches.

Sailing ship
Starting in the 1400s, European sailors explored the world in fast, sturdy ships like this one.

Four masts for large sails

Sailors spotted land from the crow's nest.

Room for cargo, food, and water.

Round Earth
In 1519 a famous Spanish explorer, Magellan, sailed around the world – and proved it was round.

Ship's compass

Finding the way
Explorers used the Sun, stars, and instruments to find their way.
Sextant
Backstaff
Telescope

Goods
Explorers brought home new foods and riches from around the world.
Jade
Cloves
Cinnamon
Pineapple

Did you know?
Before the 1520s, most people thought the world was flat!

Find out more   Vikings 145   Ships and boats 127   61

Science and Technology
This key subject area covers everything in the world of science, from the human body to space travel.

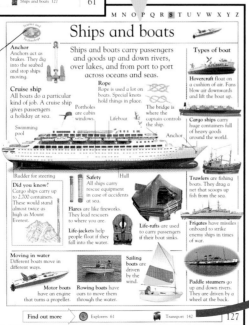

Ships and boats

Anchor
Anchors act as brakes. They dig into the seabed and stop ships moving.

Cruise ship
All boats do a particular kind of job. A cruise ship gives passengers a holiday at sea.

Portholes are cabin windows.

Swimming pool

Lifeboat

Rudder for steering   Hull

Did you know?
Cargo ships carry up to 2,700 containers. These would stand almost twice as high as Mount Everest.

Ships and boats carry passengers and goods up and down rivers, over lakes, and from port to port across oceans and seas.

Rope
Rope is used a lot on boats. Special knots hold things in place.

The **bridge** is where the captain controls the ship.

Anchor

Safety
All ships carry rescue equipment in case of accidents at sea.

Flares are like fireworks. They lead rescuers to where you are.

Life-jackets help people float if they fall into the water.

Moving in water
Different boats move in different ways.

Motor boats have an engine that turns a propeller.

Rowing boats have oars to move them through the water.

Sailing boats are driven by the wind.

Types of boat

Hovercraft float on a cushion of air. Fans blow air downwards and lift the boat up.

Cargo ships carry huge containers full of heavy goods around the world.

Trawlers are fishing boats. They drag a net that scoops up fish from the sea.

Life-rafts are used to carry passengers if their boat sinks.

Frigates have missiles onboard to strike enemy ships in times of war.

Paddle steamers go up and down rivers. They are driven by a wheel at the back.

Find out more   Explorers 61   Transport 142   127

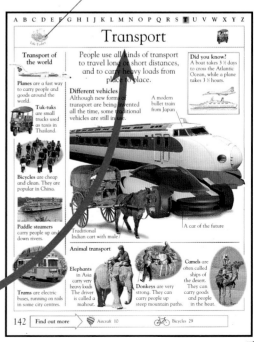

Transport

Transport of the world

Planes are a fast way to carry people and goods around the world.

Tuk-tuks are small trucks used as taxis in Thailand.

Bicycles are cheap and clean. They are popular in China.

Paddle steamers carry people up and down rivers.

Trams are electric buses, running on rails in some city centres.

People use all kinds of transport to travel long or short distances, and to carry heavy loads from place to place.

Different vehicles
Although new forms of transport are being invented all the time, some traditional vehicles are still in use.

A modern bullet train from Japan.

Traditional Indian cart with mule

A car of the future

Did you know?
A boat takes 3½ days to cross the Atlantic Ocean, while a plane takes 3½ hours.

Animal transport

Elephants in Asia carry very heavy loads. The driver is called a mahout.

Donkeys are very strong. They can carry people up steep mountain paths.

Camels are often called ships of the desert. They can carry goods and people in the heat.

142   Find out more   Aircraft 10   Bicycles 29

5

Continents of the World

Africa

Northern Africa

Northern Africa is one of the hottest parts of the world. It is made up of mountains, rainforests, and a great sweeping desert.

Atlas Mountains
These mountains form a high wall between the Sahara Desert and the wetter land on the coast.

Hoggar Mountains
These red mountains rise up out of the Sahara Desert.

River Nile
The muddy banks of the Nile make fertile farmland.

Rainforest
Rainforest grows near the equator, where there is heavy rain.

Ethiopian Highlands
The Ethiopian Highlands are hot, dry, scrubland. Farming is very difficult here.

RABAT • MOROCCO
ATLAS MOUNTAINS
• ALGIERS • TUNIS
TUNISIA
• TRIPOLI
Suez Canal
CAIRO •
River Nile
EL AAIUN •
WESTERN SAHARA
ALGERIA
LIBYA
EGYPT
S A H A R A   D E S E R T
N
HOGGAR MOUNTAINS
NOUAKCHOTT •
MAURITANIA
SENEGAL
1 •
2 • GAMBIA
3 • GUINEA BISSAU
Capital cities
1 DAKAR
2 BANJUL
3 BISSAU
4 CONAKRY
5 FREETOWN
6 MONROVIA
7 YAMOUSSOUKRO
4 • GUINEA
5 • SIERRA LEONE
LIBERIA
6 •
MALI
• BAMAKO
• OUAGADOUGOU
BURKINA
NIAMEY •
NIGER
NIGERIA
• ABUJA
IVORY COAST
TOGO
BENIN
GHANA
ACCRA
LOME
• PORTO-NOVO
7 •
CAMEROON
• YAOUNDE
CHAD
Lake Chad
N'DJAMENA •
CENTRAL AFRICAN REPUBLIC
BANGUI •
SUDAN
KHARTOUM •
ERITREA
• ASMARA
ETHIOPIAN HIGHLANDS
• ADDIS ABABA
DJIBOUTI
DJIBOUTI •
ETHIOPIA
SOMALIA
• MOGADISHU

Fennec fox
The fennec fox lives in the desert. Its huge ears give off heat, cooling the fox down.

Did you know?
- The Sahara Desert is the largest desert in the world.
- At 6,670 km (4,145 miles), the Nile is the longest river in the world.

Sahara Desert
The Sahara Desert has burning hot days and freezing cold nights. Winds blow the sand into dunes.

Lake Chad
Lake Chad is now shrinking, as the rivers that feed it begin to dry up.

Find out more   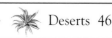 Deserts 46   Rivers and lakes 119

Continents of the World

Africa

Southern Africa

Southern Africa's thick rainforests, dry deserts, and rolling grasslands are home to a huge variety of animals and plants.

Congo rainforest
The Congo rainforest is home to a huge variety of wildlife.

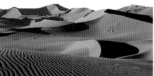

Namib Desert
This desert has towering sand dunes. It contains diamonds and precious metals.

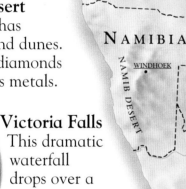

Victoria Falls
This dramatic waterfall drops over a steep cliff in the River Zambezi.

Did you know?
• The Great Rift Valley is a huge crack in the Earth's crust.
• At 5,895 m (19,340 ft), Mt. Kilimanjaro is the highest mountain in Africa.

Mount Kilimanjaro
Although this ancient volcano lies close to the equator, it is always covered in snow.

Great Rift Valley
This huge valley was formed millions of years ago. It is a land of lakes and volcanoes.

Baobab tree
These trees survive dry weather by storing water inside their trunks.

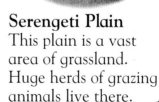

Serengeti Plain
This plain is a vast area of grassland. Huge herds of grazing animals live there.

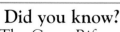

Table Mountain
This flat-topped mountain is often hidden by a cloud that locals call the 'tablecloth'.

Wildlife
No two zebras are exactly the same. Their stripes camouflage them, and help to confuse their enemies.

Map labels
MALABO
EQUATORIAL GUINEA
LIBREVILLE
GABON
CONGO
River Congo
ZAIRE
BRAZZAVILLE
Cabinda
KINSHASA
UGANDA
KAMPALA
KENYA
NAIROBI
Lake Victoria
RWANDA
KIGALI
BUJUMBURA
BURUNDI
SERENGETI PLAIN
Mount Kilimanjaro
LUANDA
DODOMA
TANZANIA
GREAT RIFT VALLEY
ANGOLA
River Zambezi
ZAMBIA
MALAWI
LILONGWE
LUSAKA
MOZAMBIQUE
NAMIBIA
Victoria Falls
HARARE
ZIMBABWE
NAMIB DESERT
WINDHOEK
BOTSWANA
GABORONE
N
MADAGASCAR
PRETORIA
MBABANE
MAPUTO
SWAZILAND
River Vaal
BLOEMFONTEIN
MASERU
LESOTHO
SOUTH AFRICA
CAPE TOWN
Table Mountain

Continents of the World

Africa: culture

Culture

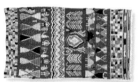

Textiles are bold and colourful. This carpet was made in Morocco.

Dance and music are an important and popular part of African village life.

Crafts, such as wood carving, are practised all over Africa.

Africa is home to millions of people. Most of them live in small villages and farm the land, but more and more are moving to the cities.

Market
Many towns in Africa have a daily market, where people gather to buy and sell goods and chat to friends.

Minerals

There are gold and diamond mines in southern and western Africa.

Tourism
Thousands of tourists visit Africa to see its magnificent landscape and wildlife.

Buyer

Farming
Many Africans still use traditional farming methods to grow food crops such as maize.

Farmer in Zimbabwe

Maize

Wheat couscous

Towns and cities
Cities all over Africa are growing quickly, as people leave their villages to look for work.

Cairo

Village houses are made with a mix of dried mud and straw baked hard in the sun.

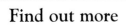

Shanty towns are home to the very poor. The shelters have no water or electricity.

Did you know?
In Chad, over 40,000 people have to share one doctor.

Find out more Towns and cities 140 Dance 44

Air

Air is a mixture of gases that swirl around the Earth. We cannot see, smell, or taste air, but it contains the oxygen we need to live and breathe.

Air pressure
Barometers measure air pressure – the weight of air pressing on the Earth.

Barometer

Air resistance
Air pushes against a parachute as it falls to Earth, and this slows it down.

Air resistance makes parachutes fall slowly.

Canopy

Harness

Parachutist

Gases in air
Humans breathe in oxygen and breathe out carbon dioxide. Plants take in carbon dioxide and put oxygen back into the air.

Air power
Hovercraft float above the sea on a cushion of air.

Mountain air
On high mountains, the air is cold and contains less oxygen.

Wind power
Wind is moving air. It can turn wind turbines, which make electricity.

Air currents
Air currents are pockets of moving air.

People use air currents for sports such as hang-gliding.

Birds use air currents to help them fly.

Plants use air currents to spread their pollen and seeds.

Did you know?
Without air, the sky would look black even during the day!

Wind speed
The Beaufort scale is used to measure the speed and strength of wind.

Light air – force 1

Gentle breeze – force 3

Strong breeze – force 6

Moderate gale – force 7

Strong gale – force 9

Find out more ➤ Energy 54 ◉ Weather 147

Aircraft

The fastest way to travel is by air. Aircraft can carry people around the world in just a few hours.

Passenger plane

Most planes today are used to carry passengers long distances. This one can carry over 100 people.

Flying instruments

Cockpit
The cockpit contains the computers and controls used by the pilot.

The fuselage is the body of the plane, where passengers sit.

Streamlined shape

Cockpit

Light aluminium body

Jet engines power the plane forwards.

Wing flaps help the plane slow down and turn in the air.

Types of aircraft

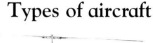

Helicopters have spinning blades called rotors.

Hot-air balloons fly because the hot air inside is lighter than the air outside.

Did you know?
The long, pointed nose of Concorde "droops", so that the pilot has a clear view for landing!

Black box
This records all the details of an aircraft's flight.

Wheels
These fold up inside the plane during the flight.

Escape chute
Air-filled chutes are the emergency exits from a plane.

Airships are filled with helium gas, which is lighter than air.

Seaplanes have floats as well as wheels. They can land on water.

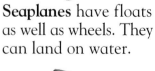

Gliders have no engine. They are towed into the sky by a plane.

Airport
Planes take off and land at airports. Cargo is brought here, and passengers wait for their flight.

Food and drink is loaded on to a plane.

Staff direct take-off and landing from the control tower.

Passengers wait in the terminal.

Find out more   Inventions 88   Transport 142

World of Nature

Amphibians

Breathing
Frogs breathe through their skin when underwater, but use their lungs on dry land.

Amphibians are animals like frogs and newts, which live partly in freshwater and partly on land. They lay their eggs in water.

Nostrils

Damp skin

Strong back legs for hopping and swimming

Large eyes look for insects.

Webbed feet move like paddles in the water.

Frog
The red-eyed tree frog is one of 4,000 different amphibians. Its body is well adapted to life both in water and on land.

Did you know?
Frogs have sticky tongues.

They flick them out to catch flies.

Deadly colour
Some amphibians, like this frog, are poisonous. Their bright colours warn other animals not to eat them.

Golden poison-arrow frog

Growing up
Amphibians change their shape as they grow. This is called metamorphosis.

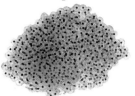

1 Large groups of frogs' eggs are called spawn.

2 Each egg grows into a tiny tadpole that takes in air through its gills.

Gills

3 The tadpole grows legs and loses its tail.

Common frog

4 The grown-up frog breathes with lungs.

Other amphibians

Marbled newt

Ornate horned toad

Fire salamander

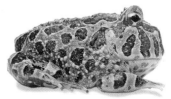

Newts have a long, thin body like a lizard.

Toads look like frogs, but have bumpy skin.

Salamanders spend most of their time on land.

Find out more ➤ Rainforest animals 113   River animals 118

Ancient China

Life in the Past

China was first formed over 2,000 years ago. Powerful emperors kept China isolated from the rest of the world.

Chinese inventions

Compasses were used at sea on Chinese ships.

Wheelbarrows were invented about 2,000 years ago.

An **earthquake detector** felt the slightest shaking of the Earth.

Paper was made from straw, rags, and water.

Silk robe

Rich people wore beautiful robes made of expensive silk.

Dragon

The dragon was an important symbol of strength and goodness. It was the emperor's symbol, too.

Ears of a bull

Demon eyes

Colourful material

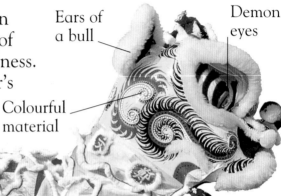

Dragon seal

Emperors used this seal to sign important papers.

Scales of a fish

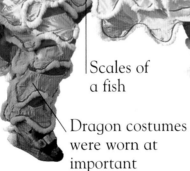

Dragon costumes were worn at important festivals.

Entertainment

The ancient Chinese loved drama and playing games, such as chess.

Chess pieces

Actor

Gambling counters

Did you know?

The Chinese used kites in the shape of a dragon to frighten the enemy in battle.

Emperor

Ancient China was ruled by emperors. The royal family was called a dynasty.

The Kangxi emperor ruled China 300 years ago.

The tomb of the first emperor was guarded by a huge army of life-size, clay soldiers.

The first emperor completed the Great Wall of China. It is still standing today.

Find out more
 Asia: culture 21
 Inventions 88

Life in the Past

Ancient Egypt

Writing
Egyptian writing was made up of rows of pictures called hieroglyphs.

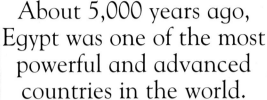

About 5,000 years ago, Egypt was one of the most powerful and advanced countries in the world.

Pyramid
The pyramids are the tombs of dead pharaohs. They were built with millions of heavy stone blocks.

Pyramids pointed to heaven

Pharaohs were buried inside.

River Nile
Egyptian farmers grew plenty of food on the banks of the Nile.

The Great Pyramid at Giza

Arts and crafts

Pottery jars and pots were made from river mud.

Pictures of everyday life were often painted on rich people's tombs.

Papyrus is a marsh reed that was made into paper.

Toys
Egyptian children played with balls and spinning tops.

Afterlife
Egyptians believed in life after death. So dead bodies were carefully preserved. These are called mummies.

Cats were very important in Egypt. They were preserved, too.

Metal, such as bronze, was used to make items like mirrors and razors.

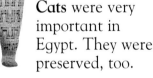

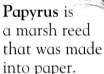

Did you know?
Dead pharaohs were buried with food and drink to help them on their journey into the next life!

Pharaoh
The kings and queens of Egypt were called pharaohs. They were thought to be gods.

Queen Nefertiti   King Tutankhamun

Lucky charms   Pendant

Jewellery was worn by the wealthy. It was often made of gold.

Find out more → Africa 6   Buildings 35

Life in the Past

Ancient Greece

Gods
The Greeks had many gods. Zeus was king of the gods.

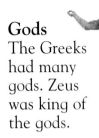
Zeus

Temple
The Greeks built wonderful stone temples to their gods. The Parthenon is 2,500 years old.

The ancient Greeks lived over 2,500 years ago, but many of their ideas are still important to us today.

Stone carvings

Mirror
This beautiful bronze mirror is decorated with a picture of Aphrodite, the goddess of beauty.

Arts and crafts

Theatre was very popular. The Greeks wrote many plays.

Pottery vases were made of red clay, and then decorated.

Carved columns

Marble columns

Toys for children were made of painted clay.

Metals were made into statues and jewellery.

Gold earring

Family life
Ancient Greek families were very close. Marriages were often arranged.

Food
Many ancient Greeks ate bread, eggs, fresh fish and figs.

Fresh figs

Fresh fish

Did you know?
Masks and platform shoes were worn in ancient Greek theatre when actors played the parts of gods.

Education
Boys went to school. They learnt music, reading, and writing.

Two boys are pictured reading books on this jug.

Musical instruments

Socrates was a famous teacher and thinker. His ideas are still read today.

Statue of Socrates

Olympics
The Greeks loved sports. They invented the Olympic Games.

Painting of athletes

14

Find out more

Religions 115   Sports of the world 136

World of Nature

Animal families

Every animal has a different kind of family life. Some animals live alone and just come together to mate. Others live in family groups.

Did you know?
Male black widow spiders are often eaten by their bigger female mate!

Lion
Lions live in family groups called prides. They share out the food between them.

Lionesses do most of the hunting.

Male lions protect the group.

Domestic cat
Unlike lions, domestic cats live alone.

All the females look after the cubs.

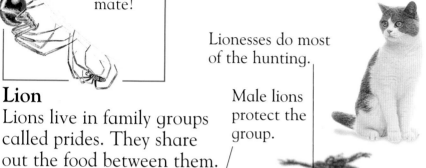

Family groups

Humans often live in a small group called a nuclear family.

Meerkats live in a large group called an extended family.

Sharks live on their own, coming together briefly to mate.

Looking after baby
Male **rheas** take care of the female's eggs, then look after their babies for a few months.

Scorpions carry their babies on their backs.

Baby **bats** are looked after in one large group called a nursery.

Baby **birds** are fed by both parents until they leave the nest.

Flycatcher

Some **fish** protect their babies by carrying them in their mouths.

Cichlid

Find out more Animal homes 16    Living things 91

World of Nature

Animal homes

Some animals make homes, others find temporary shelter. Whether animals live alone or in groups, their homes protect them from danger or bad weather.

Different homes

Hermit crabs make their homes in an empty seashell.

Squirrels make warm homes called dreys from twigs and leaves.

Clownfish live among the stinging tentacles of sea anemones.

Tortoises have mobile homes – their hard shells protect them.

Marmosets make a different home every night in the treetops.

Rabbit warren
Wild rabbits live together in a warren – a system of underground tunnels and rooms.

Entrance is dug into the earth or among tree roots.

When baby rabbits grow up they also live in the warren.

Baby rabbits live in nests called stops.

Underground rooms called burrows

Termite nest
Termites build amazing nests housing up to five million termites.

Network of cells and tunnels made from dried mud.

Some nests are 12 m (40 ft) tall!

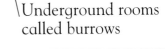

Did you know?
A female polar bear and her cubs sleep all winter in a warm den under the snow.

Find out more

Animal families 15
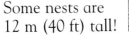
Eggs and nests 51

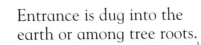

World of Nature

Animals

Mammals, such as humans, live mainly on land. Only a few live in the sea.

There are over ten million different species of animal in the world. Scientists have divided them into two main groups.

Did you know?
Most invertebrates are so tiny they can only be seen under a microscope.

Vertebrates

Fish live in the world's rivers, lakes, and seas. They take in oxygen through their gills.

Invertebrates

Starfish and sea urchins belong to a group of animals with spiny skins.

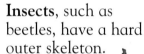

Octopuses and squid have soft bodies. They are related to molluscs, but do not have a shell.

Amphibians, such as frogs and toads, live both on land and in water.

Reptiles, such as snakes, lay their eggs on land, and have dry, scaly skins.

Molluscs, such as snails, have hard shells to protect them from enemies and the Sun.

Insects, such as beetles, have a hard outer skeleton.

Birds are animals with beaks, feathers, and wings. Most of them can fly.

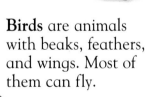

Crustaceans, such as crabs, shed their shells when they grow too big for them. A new shell grows underneath.

Vertebrates

Vertebrates are animals with backbones. They are split into five main groups.

Invertebrates

Invertebrates are animals with no backbones. Many have hard shells or a tough outer skeleton to protect them.

Find out more
 Living things 91
 Skeletons 128

Animals in danger

Large copper butterflies are very nearly extinct because their marshy habitat is being destroyed.

All over the world, wild animals are in danger. Some are killed for their skins, others live in areas called habitats that are being destroyed. These animals need our protection.

Protecting animals

Large nature reserves give animals like elephants the space they need to live.

Habitat destruction
Wild animals can die out due to lack of food and shelter if their habitat is destroyed.

Orang-utans' rainforest habitats are being destroyed as trees are cut down to make way for farming.

Zoos help rare animals like eagles breed. The young can then be released into the wild.

Hunting
Wild cats, snakes, and crocodiles are hunted for their beautiful skins, as well as other parts of their bodies.

Tigers are in danger of dying out because they are killed for their claws and teeth used in Chinese medicines.

Snakes are killed in their thousands to make snakeskin bags and shoes.

Laws ban rare animals such as tortoises from being sold as pets.

Did you know?
There are less than 200 pandas left in China's forests.

Pollution
Factory waste and farm chemicals can pollute the land, air, and water, poisoning many wild animals.

Seals can die from diseases caught from the polluted water in which they live.

Laws ban goods made from the skins of certain animals, like crocodiles.

Find out more 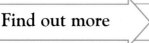 Asia 24 Conservation 43

Continents of the World

Antarctica

Antarctica is a vast, ice-covered continent near the South Pole. No one lives here permanently. It is the coldest and windiest place on Earth.

Did you know?
- Antarctica is bigger than Europe and the USA put together.
- Antarctica is actually a desert! It has no rain all year round.

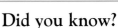

Research station

Antarctic summer
In some places, the ice melts in summer. But the ground remains frozen.

QUEEN MAUD LAND

ANTARCTIC PENINSULA

ELLSWORTH MOUNTAINS

ENDERBY LAND

MARIE BYRD LAND

TRANSANTARCTIC MOUNTAINS

◆ South Pole

ROSS ICE SHELF

ANTARCTICA

WILKES LAND

Scientists
Scientists from around the world visit Antarctica to study the land and its wildlife.

Iceberg
Icebergs are huge chunks of ice that break off from the land and float in the sea.

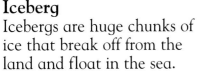

Tourism
Tourists admire Antarctica's scenery from large cruise ships.

South pole
The south pole is the most southerly point on the Earth.

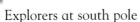

Explorers at south pole

Minerals
Below the ice and rock lie coal, copper, gold, and other valuable materials.

Wildlife
Some animals and a few simple plants have adapted to life in Antarctica. The animals hunt for food in the sea.

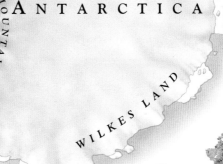

Albatross

Penguins

Moss

Leopard seal

Find out more ▷ Explorers 61   Polar lands 112

Continents of the World

Asia

Eastern Asia
Eastern Asia is a vast area, which has many great rivers, dry deserts, windy highlands, and flat, grassy plains.

Rafflesia plant
This flower is the largest in the world.

Mount Fuji
Mount Fuji is Japan's highest and most beautiful mountain.

Yangtze River
The Yangtze river in China is the third longest river in the world.

ULAN BATOR •

MONGOLIA
GOBI DESERT

TAKLA MAKAN DESERT

C H I N A

NORTH KOREA
• PYONGYANG
• SEOUL
SOUTH KOREA

JAPAN

TOKYO
▲ Mount Fuji

BEIJING •

Yellow River

TIBET

Yangtze River

GUANGXI ZHUANG

TAIPEI
TAIWAN

BURMA
• HANOI
VIETNAM
VIENTIANE
LAOS
RANGOON
THAILAND
Hainan

HONG KONG
MACAO

Luzon

Tibet
Tibet is so high above sea level that it is known as the roof of the world.

BANGKOK •

CAMBODIA
• PHNOM PENH

• MANILA

PHILIPPINES

Gobi Desert
The rocky Gobi Desert is very hot in summer, but cold and windy in winter.

Mindanao

BRUNEI

Mangrove swamps
Mangrove trees grow along the coasts of the region's islands.

MALAYSIA
KUALA LUMPUR
BANDAR SERI BEGAWAN

• SINGAPORE

Sumatra

Borneo

Celebes

Moluccas

Irian Jaya

Thailand's coastline
Parts of the Thai coastline have strange rocky towers and steep cliff faces.

Did you know?
• There are more volcanoes in east Asia than anywhere else in the world
• The country of Indonesia is made up of over 13,000 islands.

N

JAKARTA
Java

I N D O N E S I A

Rainforest
Thick tropical rainforest grow on the hillsides of many of the islands.

Panda
Pandas live in the mountains of China. They feed on bamboo leaves.

Find out more Mammals of the world 95 Rainforests 114

Continents of the World

Asia: culture

Eastern Asia
Many people in eastern Asia live on quiet farms. Others work in high-tech factories in busy cities.

Did you know?
In Japan, people are employed to push passengers on to crowded tube trains!

Industry, Japan
Japan is a world leader in producing televisions and other electrical and high-technology goods.

Television production line

Electronic circuitry board

Population
One-fifth of the world's population lives in China.

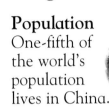

Factory workers

Culture
Buddhism is a very important religion in much of southeast Asia.

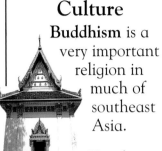

Temple

Shadow puppets have been popular entertainment in Indonesia for hundreds of years.

Lacquered goods, such as this plate, are made in Thailand.

Kimonos are traditional Japanese dress. These gowns are made from silk.

Village life
Many of the Asian people live in small, country villages. They farm the land in traditional ways.

Rubber trees
In Malaysia, the sap from rubber trees is collected and turned into rubber.

Food and drink
Rice, tea, and wheat are grown in the region. Fresh fish is a very important food.

Jasmine tea

Rice

Raw fish dish

Korean dish

Folk music is very popular. The nomads of Mongolia sing to the music of a fiddle.

Fiddle

Find out more   Factories 62   Theatre 139

Continents of the World

Asia

Northern Asia
Northern Asia stretches from the frozen lands in the north to the rolling grasslands and barren deserts in the south.

Did you know?
- The Caspian Sea is the largest lake in the world. It is four times the size of Portugal.
- Lake Baikal is the oldest and deepest lake on Earth.

Siberia
In the north of Asia, there is a vast, snow-covered area called Siberia.

Iris
The Siberian iris flowers in the summer months.

Ural mountains
These mountains have been worn down by the weather over hundreds of years.

Tundra
Much of Siberia is a frozen, treelesss plain called the tundra.

BELORUSSIA
MINSK

UKRAINE

KIEV
• MOSCOW

BLACK SEA

River Volga

URAL MOUNTAINS

RUSSIAN FEDERATION
SIBERIA

River Lena

River Kolyma

KAMCHATKA

GEORGIA
ARMENIA 1
2

AZERBAIJAN 3

CASPIAN SEA

KAZAKHSTAN

River Ob'

River Yenisey

STANOVOY RANGE

Capital cities
1 TBILISI
2 YEREVAN
3 BAKU
4 ASHGABAT
5 DUSHANBE
6 TASHKENT
7 BISHKEK
8 ALMATY

TURKMENISTAN

UZBEKISTAN

ARAL SEA

Lake Balkhash

TAJIKISTAN
KYRGYSTAN
5 6
7 8

Lake Baikal

River Volga
The River Volga flows over 3,500 km (2,000 miles) into the Caspian sea.

Aral sea
This large saltwater lake lies in dry, desert land.

Husky dogs
In Siberia, people use huskies to pull sledges across the snow.

Lake Baikal
Lake Baikal is fed by over 300 rivers, and is home to many rare animals.

Find out more 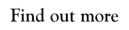 Polar animals 111   Polar lands 112

Continents of the World

Asia: culture

Did you know?

In winter, Siberian children stand under sun lamps. It's meant to keep them healthy.

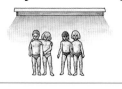

Northern Asia

The Russian Federation is the biggest country in the world, with many different peoples and cultures.

Regional food

Borscht is a famous soup made from beetroot. It comes from the Ukraine.

Caviar, the eggs of the sturgeon fish, is a very expensive delicacy.

Trans-Siberian railway

This railway is the longest in the world. It reaches from one side of the country to the other.

Kremlin, Moscow

The Kremlin was once home to the Russian Tsars. It now houses the government.

Assumption Cathedral

Archangel Cathedral

Grand Kremlin Palace

Bread forms an essential part of the Russian diet.

Industry

Heavy industries, like iron and steel making, have led to problems with air pollution in the region.

Mining is very important. Coal, gold, and diamonds are all mined here.

Sulphur

Coal

Draniki is the national dish of Belorussia. It is made from grated potatoes.

Craftwork

Fur hat

Silk scarf

Russian dolls

Balalaika

Russian peoples

Russian peoples, such as the Cossacks and the Kyrgyz nomads, all have special customs and different traditions

Russian Cossacks

Kyrgyz nomads

Find out more Rocks and minerals 120   Transport 142

Continents of the World

Asia

Western and southern Asia
Some of the world's hottest deserts and highest mountains lie in this part of the Asian continent.

Did you know?
- About one-third of the world's oil is found in western and southern Asia.
- Indian elephants have smaller ears than African elephants.

Hot pools
These amazing hot pools in Turkey are made of minerals.

Desert
Sandy desert covers most of Saudi Arabia.

Capital cities
1 NICOSIA
2 BEIRUT
3 JERUSALEM
4 MANAMA
5 DOHA
6 ABU DHABI
7 MUSCAT

Indian elephant
Elephants live in the forests of India.

Mount Everest
Mount Everest, in the Himalayas, is the highest mountain in the world.

BLACK SEA
ANKARA
TURKEY
CYPRUS 1
LEBANON
2
ISRAEL
3
AMMAN
JORDAN
SYRIA
DAMASCUS
IRAQ
BAGHDAD
CASPIAN SEA
TEHRAN
IRAN
AFGHANISTAN
KABUL
ISLAMABAD
PAKISTAN
KASHMIR
River Indus
NEPAL
Mount Everest
THIMPHU
KATHMANDU
BHUTAN
NEW DELHI
KUWAIT
KUWAIT CITY
SAUDI
ARABIA
BAHRAIN
4
QATAR
5
RIYADH
6
UNITED
ARAB
EMIRATES
7
RED SEA
EMPTY
QUARTER
SAN'A
YEMEN
OMAN
River Ganges
BANGLADESH
DACCA
INDIA
N
SRI LANKA
COLOMBO

Wadi
Desert rivers often dry up, leaving rocky river-beds called wadis.

Red Sea
The Red Sea divides northern Africa from western Asia.

River Ganges
This river carries water to a large part of India and Bangladesh.

Kashmir
Kashmir is a land of lakes and mountains.

Sri Lanka
The island of Sri Lanka is fringed with white, sandy beaches.

Find out more   Mountains 99   Oil 106

Continents of the World

Asia: culture

Products

Jute is grown in Bangladesh to make sacking and rope.

Oranges and other citrus fruits are grown in Israel.

Tea is grown on large plantations in India and Sri Lanka.

Oil is drilled in the desert countries in the west.

Bollywood, Bombay
This is the centre of India's film industry.

Western and southern Asia
Most people still live in small villages, but many are moving to the cities for work.

Taj Mahal, Agra
This marble tomb in India was built as a memorial to the wife of an emperor. It is over 350 years old.

Delicate design

Beautiful towers on both sides

White marble walls

Riyadh
The city of Riyadh in Saudi Arabia was built with money from oil. All its buildings are new.

Food
Spices and fruit are used to flavour many dishes.

Cinnamon   Coriander   Turmeric

Apricots   Dates   Garlic

Nomads
Nomads still live in parts of Asia, moving from place to place.

Craftwork
The craftwork in this part of Asia is brightly coloured and highly decorated.

Child's hat

Indian dress

Sitar

Turkish rug

Did you know?
In Bhutan, archery competitors jump in front of the targets to distract each other!

Find out more   Film 66   Foods of the world 71

Continents of the World

Australasia

Australia and Papua New Guinea
From mountains and rainforests, to deserts and coral reefs, Australasia has a varied landscape and unique wildlife.

Did you know?
- Australia has many animals that live nowhere else in the world.
- The Great Barrier Reef is the largest living structure on Earth.

Blue Mountains
The Blue Mountains run down the eastern coast of Australia.

Rainforest
Tropical rainforest covers over two-thirds of Papua New Guinea.

Desert rocks
These strange desert rocks in western Australia are called the Pinnacles.

Great Barrier Reef
The Great Barrier Reef is a long line of reefs and islands. It is made of living coral.

N

PAPUA NEW GUINEA
• PORT MORESBY

ARNHEM LAND

NORTHERN TERRITORY

GREAT SANDY DESERT

A U S T R A L I A

MACDONNELL RANGES

GIBSON DESERT

Uluru (Ayers Rock)

WESTERN AUSTRALIA

GREAT VICTORIA DESERT

SOUTH AUSTRALIA

QUEENSLAND

GREAT BARRIER REEF

GREAT DIVIDING RANGE

River Darling

NEW SOUTH WALES

River Murray

CANBERRA

VICTORIA

AUSTRALIAN CAPITAL TERRITORY

BLUE MOUNTAINS

TASMANIA

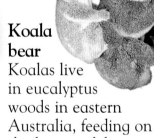

Koala bear
Koalas live in eucalyptus woods in eastern Australia, feeding on the leaves of the trees.

Outback
The middle of Australia is dry grassland, known as the outback.

Tasmanian devil
This fierce animal has sharp teeth and a nasty snarl. It lives only in Tasmania.

Uluru (Ayers rock)
This huge rock in the desert is a sacred place for Aboriginals, the first people of Australia.

Tasmania
Tasmania is a small island that lies south of Australia.

Find out more Birds of the world 31 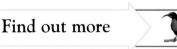 Seas and oceans 124

Continents of the World

Australasia

New Zealand and Pacific Islands

Hot springs, volcanoes, and white, sandy beaches are just some of the features of New Zealand and the Pacific islands.

Did you know?
- New Zealand's most beautiful areas are protected as national parks.
- There are about 30,000 islands in the Pacific Ocean.

PACIFIC ISLANDS

Solomon Islands

New Caledonia

Vanuatu

Fiji

Fiji
Fiji is made up of 322 islands. Much of the land is covered with forest and surrounded by coral reefs.

N

Kiwi

Kiwi birds cannot fly. They live in New Zealand.

NORTH ISLAND

Lake Taupo

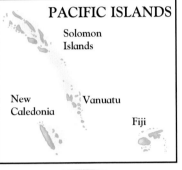

Mount Cook
Mount Cook is the highest mountain in New Zealand.

Tropical island
The Pacific islands have long, sandy beaches, and sparkling blue seas.

SOUTH ISLAND

• WELLINGTON

Mud pools
Heat from inside the Earth makes hot mud pools in New Zealand.

Geyser
Geysers are hot water fountains that shoot out of the ground.

Fjord
New Zealand's coastline has deep inlets called fjords.

SOUTHERN ALPS

NEW ZEALAND

Mount Cook

Lake Wakatipu

Lake Te Anau

Kakapo
This New Zealand parrot is very rare. It is too heavy to fly.

Stewart Island

Sheep
The wet climate provides good grazing for sheep.

Volcano
There are many active volcanoes in New Zealand.

Lake
Beautiful, freshwater lakes fill the craters in the mountains.

Find out more Birds of the world 31   Seas and oceans 124

Continents of the World

Australasia: culture

The people of Australasia have different lifestyles. Some still lead a traditional life, far from the nearest town. Others live busy lives in modern, crowded cities.

Sports
Rugby is a very popular sport in Fiji.

Tribes
There are over 1,000 different tribes in Papua New Guinea.

Farming

Wool from the sheep farms is sent all over the world.

Sydney Opera House
This modern opera house overlooks Sydney harbour. Most cities in Australia are on the coast.

White-tiled roofs

The arched roofs look like the sails of yachts.

Sydney harbour

Orange   Tamarillo

Peach

Fruit farming suits New Zealand's warm, wet climate.

Mining
Mining is important. Gold, gemstones, coal, iron, and copper are all mined in Australia.

Gold   Opal

Tourism
The stunning scenery and relaxing lifestyle attract many tourists.

Did you know?
Some Australian farms are so large, farmers use planes to get across them.

Aboriginal and Maori people

Aboriginal people settled in Australia more than 50,000 years ago.

Aboriginal bark painting

Maori people came to New Zealand over 1,000 years ago.

Maori carving

Find out more   Farm animals 63   Painting 107

Science and Technology

Bicycles

Bikes are a popular kind of transport because they are cheap, clean, easy to repair, and keep us healthy. Add an engine, and you have a motorbike.

Did you know?
The record number of people to ride one motorbike is 46.

Bicycle
Bikes are machines. They are moved by cyclists pushing the pedals round with their feet.

Tyres are filled with air so that they roll over bumps.

Saddle

Handlebars steer the bike.

Frame

Spokes

Pedals

Brakes stop the bike.

Gears give cyclists more power.

Chain links pedals to back wheel.

Pannier
Panniers can be fixed to a bike to carry things.

Riding a bicycle
Learning to ride a bike is a tricky skill. It needs a good sense of balance.

Types of bicycle

Road bikes are light but strong for use on bumpy roads.

Rickshaws are used as taxis to carry passengers around.

Unicycles are often seen in circuses. Balancing on one wheel is difficult!

Tripletandems are for three riders. They have three seats and three sets of pedals!

Cantilevers are the most modern racing bikes. They have streamlined frames.

Motorbike
Motorbikes are more complicated machines than bikes. They are driven by powerful engines.

Engine Fuel tank

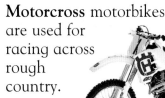

Scooters have small engines. They are popular for travelling around town.

Motorcross motorbikes are used for racing across rough country.

Find out more ➤ Cars 37 ✂ Machines 92

Birds

Birds come in all shapes and sizes and are the only animals with feathers. They have a beak but no teeth, and their babies hatch out of eggs.

Did you know?
The ostrich is too heavy to fly, but runs fast instead!

A bird has wings instead of arms.

Tail is used for balance.

Ears are hidden under feathers.

The shape of a bird's beak tells you what it eats.

Eyes are sharp to spot food.

Robin
Like most birds, this robin has a light, streamlined body, which helps it to fly.

Leg

Claws grip branches and grab food.

Beaks and food

Hummingbirds suck nectar with their long beaks.

Parrots crack open hard nuts with their beaks.

Eagles kill small animals with their sharp beaks.

Flamingoes scoop up algae and tiny fish.

Finches peck at seeds and nuts.

Feathers
Long tail and wing feathers are used for flight and balance. While the soft, downy chest feathers keep a bird warm.

Chest feathers

Wing feathers

Flying
A bird stays up in the air by flapping its strong wings. Some birds can glide on the wind.

The feathers close up and push down against the air.

As the wings rise, the feathers spread apart.

Pigeon

Find out more 〉 Birds of the world 31   Eggs and nests 51

World of Nature

Birds of the world

There are more than 8,500 different birds, and they live in every part of the world. Each bird's body and feeding habits have adapted to suit where it lives.

Did you know?
The rhinoceros hornbill has a box on its beak that makes its call so loud, it can be heard over 2 km (1 mile) away.

Barn owl
The barn owl lives in northern Europe, feeding on small mammals.

Bald eagle
The bald eagle, found in North America, swoops down to grab its prey.

Shelduck
The shelduck feeds on small shellfish. It is found on river estuaries and mudflats in central Asia.

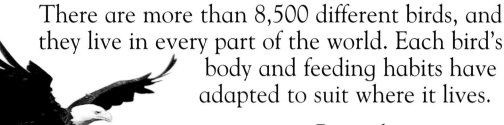

ARCTIC OCEAN
EUROPE
ASIA
NORTH AMERICA
PACIFIC OCEAN
ATLANTIC OCEAN
AFRICA
SOUTH AMERICA
INDIAN OCEAN
AUSTRALASIA
ANTARCTICA

Toucan
Toucans live in the hot, steamy rainforests of South America, eating tropical fruit.

Kiwi
Kiwis can't fly. They live only in New Zealand.

Scarlet macaw
Macaws live on the edge of South American rainforests, eating fruit, nuts, and seeds.

Sunbirds
Native to Africa, scarlet-chested sunbirds eat insects and nectar.

Cockatoo
Living on the Australian grasslands, cockatoos feed on seeds and leaves.

Emperor penguin
Penguins live in icy cold Antarctica. They can't fly, but are excellent swimmers.

Flamingo
Many flamingos live in the hot lakes of Africa. They feed on tiny shrimps and algae.

Find out more Birds 30 Eggs and nests 51

Life Today

Books

The words and pictures inside books provide readers with information, ideas, and fun.

Library
Public libraries are places where people can read and borrow many different kinds of books.

Novelty books
Novelty books have pop-ups, flaps, and stickers to make reading fun.

Book shelves | Study desk

Non-fiction

Non-fiction books are about the real world. They contain facts, pictures, and photographs.

Fiction
Fiction books contain made-up stories. Children's fiction often has pictures.

CD Roms
CD Roms are information discs read by computers. They have pictures, words, and sounds.

Writing
To write, people use a collection of letters and symbols called an alphabet.

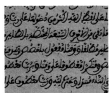
The **Chinese** use symbols called characters.

Arabic words read from right to left.

The **Roman alphabet** is used around the world.

Braille books
Braille books use a special alphabet of raised dots that blind people "read" with their fingers.

Find out more → Ancient Greece 14    Human body: senses 81

Bridges and tunnels

Types of bridge

Brenner Bridge

Beam bridges are supported by strong columns called piers.

Québec Railway Bridge

Cantilever bridges balance the deck on strong supports.

Tyne Bridge

Arch bridges push their weight into the banks of the river.

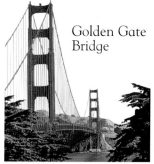

Golden Gate Bridge

Suspension bridges hang from cables held up by towers.

Everywhere we go there are obstacles to cross. Bridges and tunnels make it easy to travel over or under rivers, across valleys, and through mountains.

Forth Rail Bridge, Scotland

The deck of this cantilever bridge is made of two pieces built out from the banks.

Support tower

Deck of bridge

Steel girders

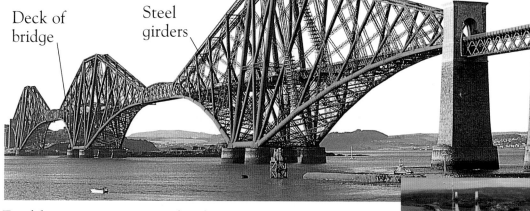

Building a suspension bridge

1 Huge cranes build tall columns, called piers, on each side of the river.

2 The towers are built. These are the strongest part of the bridge.

3 Pieces of deck are hung from the strong, steel cables.

Tunnel

Tunnels burrow under barriers such as mountains, seas, and crowded city streets.

Road tunnel through a mountain.

Train coming out of a tunnel under the sea.

Huge drilling machines bore tunnels through the hard rock.

Find out more Building machines 34   Europe: culture 56

Science and Technology

Building machines

In the past, many great buildings were built by hand and took years to complete. Today's powerful machines make building work much quicker and easier.

Did you know?
It would take one man two months to do the same work a backhoe loader does in one hour!

Bulldozer
A bulldozer clears and flattens the ground ready for building.

Big steel bucket pushes earth aside.

Hand-held machines
Not all machines on building sites are huge trucks. Some are much smaller machines.

Exhaust pipe

Driver's cab

Crawler tracks can move over rough ground.

Pneumatic drill

Cement mixer

Wheelbarrow

Types of building machine

Concrete mixers bring ready-mixed concrete to a site.

Excavators dig out trenches, where pipes and foundations are laid.

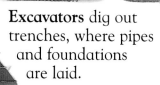

Tipper trucks bring all the building materials to a site.

Backhoe loaders dig trenches and then remove the rubble.

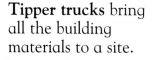

Building site
Many machines are used on building sites. They are busy and dangerous places to work.

Crane

Concrete mixer

Demolition ball
Demolition balls smash down old buildings so that new ones can be built in their place.

Truck-loader cranes lift heavy loads to the top of a building.

Find out more ▷ Buildings 35 ✂ Machines 92

Science and Technology

Buildings

Every building has a purpose – whether it's for leisure, worship, or work. But every one is different – built from a mix of materials in a variety of styles.

Did you know?
Tall skyscrapers are built to sway slightly in strong winds.

Place of worship
St Basil's Cathedral in Russia was built to celebrate a victory in war. Today, it is used as a museum.

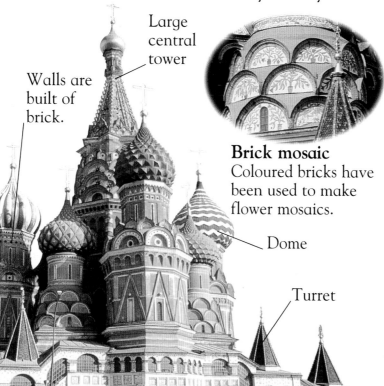

Large central tower

Walls are built of brick.

Brick mosaic
Coloured bricks have been used to make flower mosaics.

Dome

Turret

Uses of buildings
Offices are built in town and city centres, where many people go to work.

Chrysler Building

Sydney Opera House
Theatre and opera houses are buildings with large seating halls inside.

Adobe houses

Houses are different around the world, and are built of a variety of materials.

Beachy Head lighthouse

Lighthouses are built to warn ships of rocky coasts and sandbanks.

Building materials
Builders use materials that are strong, weatherproof, and easy to get hold of.

Wooden beams hold up the floors and ceilings.

Tiles on the roof keep out the rain. They are made of clay.

Bricks are stuck together in rows to build walls.

Thatch is made of reeds or straw. It makes a waterproof roof.

World of Nature

Butterflies and moths

With their colourful wings, butterflies are the most beautiful insects. Moths are less colourful because most of them fly at night.

A butterfly's mouth, called a proboscis, is like a long, curly straw.

Scaly wings

Butterflies smell with their antennae.

Head

Defence
Eyespots on the wings of this butterfly frighten enemies away.

Banana eater

This butterfly camouflages itself by pretending to be a leaf.

Leaf butterfly

Thorax / Abdomen

Swallowtail butterfly
Butterflies and moths are insects. Like this swallowtail, they all have three body parts, six legs, and four large wings.

Growing up

1 Butterfly eggs hatch out into caterpillars.

2 A caterpillar grows so fast, it must keep shedding its skin.

3 The fully grown caterpillar slowly makes a hard case called a chrysalis.

4 About four weeks later, a butterfly crawls out and dries its wings.

Citrus swallowtail

Moth facts

Thick, furry body

Large, feathery antennae

Wings spread out when resting

Butterfly facts

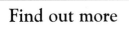

Slender body

Smooth antennae with club-like ends

Wings folded when resting

Did you know?
This African moth has a proboscis three times as long as its body to suck nectar from exotic flowers.

Find out more Insects 86 Spiders and minibeasts 134

Cars

Cars come in all shapes and sizes and are used by all sorts of people. The job a car does affects its looks, its performance, and its price!

Airbag
Airbags fill up with air to protect people in a crash.

Family car
Engineers use computers to create the best design for a particular car, such as this family estate.

Baby car seat
Babies sit in small seats with straps to keep them safe.

Large luggage space

Five comfortable passenger seats

Streamlined shape

Small engine cuts down on fuel.

Types of car

Classic cars are old, stylish cars that have survived from early years of motoring.

Police cars are fitted with radios, sirens, and other special equipment.

Customized cars have been chopped up, added to, and painted to make them look unusual.

Wheel

Indicators warn other drivers when the car is going to turn.

Mirror
Car mirrors help drivers to see the road behind them.

All-terrain vehicles have powerful engines. Big wheels keep a grip on muddy tracks.

Tyre
Different cars use different kinds of tyre.

Did you know?
The world's longest car has 26 wheels and a tiny swimming pool on board!

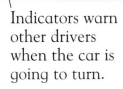

Road tyre   Racing car tyre

Battery-run car
This car is for a disabled driver. It is much cleaner because it runs on a battery, not on petrol.

Racing cars only have room for the driver. They are low, streamlined, and fast.

Find out more   Factories 62    Trucks 144

Castles

Did you know?
The world's largest castle is in Prague, Czech Republic. It has a cathedral inside!

Castles were once the homes of kings and lords. These strong buildings protected them from their enemies.

Types of castle

Saumur castle lies on the banks of the River Loire in France. It has tall, pointed towers.

Flag
The flag carries the lord's coat of arms.

Drawbridge
Pulling up the drawbridge cut the castle off from enemies.

Caerphilly castle is the largest castle in Wales. It was built between 1268–1271.

Spanish castle
This castle has two sets of thick stone walls. It was built in 1475 and became a luxury palace.

El Real de Manzanares

Turrets

Arrow loop
Archers fired arrows through slits in the walls.

Battlements

Portcullis
A metal grille protected the wooden gates.

Krak des Chevaliers was a huge crusader fortress. It could house over 2,000 soldiers.

Neuschwanstein looks like a fairy-tale castle. It was built in Germany in the 1800s.

Laying siege
In a siege, an enemy army surrounded a castle and attacked it with powerful weapons.

Giant catapults hurled rocks and stones at the castle walls.

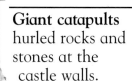

Crossbows
fired arrows at soldiers on the castle battlements.

Cannons began to be used in about 1350.

Archers with crossbows kept up the attack.

George du dades castle in Morocco had very high walls. It was hard to attack.

World of Nature

Climates

Every part of the world has its own climate, a pattern of weather that is roughly the same every year, and affects the plants that grow there.

Cold forest spruce

Scotland

Namibia

Cold forest climate
This has long, snowy winters, and short, cool summers.

Desert climate
A desert climate is very dry. Most deserts have burning hot days and freezing cold nights.

Desert cactus

Malaysia

Tropical climate
This climate is hot all year round. There is heavy rain every day for many months of the year.

Rainforest leaf

England

Temperate climate
This climate has warm summers and cool winters. It rains most months of the year.

Temperate leaf

Antarctica

Polar climate
Polar climates are cold and icy all year round. They are also very dry.

Polar lichen

What affects the climate?

The land
The higher you climb, the colder it gets. High places, such as mountains, have colder climates.

The Sun
The Sun is hotter near the Equator and cooler at the poles. A place is hot or cold depending on where it lies.

The sea
Places near the sea have milder climates than places inland. The summers are cool, the winters are mild.

Science and Technology

Colour

A world without colour would be a dull place. The beautiful colours around us are actually different kinds of light.

Sunlight
Although sunlight looks white, it is actually made up of many different colours. You can see these colours in a rainbow.

_____ Red

_____ Orange

_____ Yellow

_____ Green

_____ Blue

_____ Indigo

_____ Violet

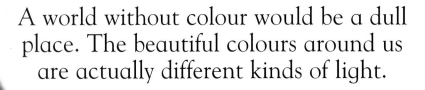

Seeing in colour
When rays of light hit this painting, some of the colours in the light are soaked up. Others bounce up into our eyes.

Primary colours
The primary colours are red, blue, and yellow. By mixing these, any other colour can be made.

Paint
Paints were once made from natural materials.

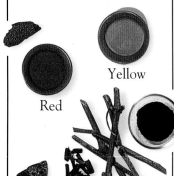

Red

Yellow

Black

Blue

Rocks or plants were crushed to make a coloured powder. This was mixed with oil.

Today, most of the paints we use have been made from chemicals.

Life without colour
Colours affect our feelings about things. Which of these meals would you rather eat?

Colour in nature
Colours help animals to communicate. This frog's bright colours warn that it is poisonous.

Peacocks attract mates with their colourful feathers.

Did you know?
Chameleons change colour when they feel angry, frightened or too hot or cold.

Find out more ▷ Light 90   Painting 107

Communications

Sign language
Some deaf people use a system of hand signals to communicate with each other.

Talking
When people talk to each other they use their voices, facial expressions, and hands to help say what they mean.

Telephone
Mobile phones turn voices into radio waves that are sent around the world by satellites.

Talking, writing, and reading are all ways in which people share their thoughts and ideas. This is known as communication.

We look at each other when we talk.

Did you know?
Native Americans used smoke signals to communicate quickly across long distances.

One-way communication

Televisions pick up radio waves and change them into sounds and pictures.

Radios pick up sound waves that travel invisibly through the air.

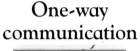

Internet
The internet is a world-wide computer system that people use to exchange messages.

Videophone
This phone has a TV picture of the person at the other end.

Writing
The earliest writing was carved on stone. Now we can print words quickly and easily.

Letters are delivered around the world by planes, trains, vans, and people.

Magazines and newspapers are a popular way of spreading information.

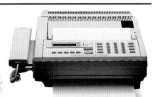

Fax machines use phone lines to send documents to other fax machines.

Science and Technology

Computers

Calculator
A calculator is a small computer that can work out complicated sums very fast.

Computers don't just sit on desks. They are the superfast electronic brains behind many of the machines we use in everyday life.

Flight simulator
Pilots train in simulators on the ground. Computers make it look as if they are flying in the air.

Virtual reality
With virtual reality machines you can imagine you are at the controls of a supersonic jet or spacecraft.

Headset has a mini-TV screen.

As you move your head, different images appear on the TV screen.

Controls

Film
In many films, computers are used to create amazing special effects.

Games
Computer games are just for fun.

Robot
Robots do many different jobs in factories. In car factories, computers "tell" robots how to assemble a car.

Motors rock the machine to make the "journey" more realistic.

Design
Designers use computers to create pictures of their ideas, such as a new car.

Personal computer
These computers can be used in many ways, from playing games to doing homework.

Screen

Hard disc

Keyboard

Chips are the "brain" of a computer.

A hard disc stores information inside the computer.

A laptop is a personal computer that you can carry around.

Did you know?
The first computer was so big it filled up a whole room!

Find out more Inventions 88   Space travel 133

Conservation

Conservation means looking after the Earth's resources – plants, animals, air, water, and land. It's a world problem, but one that begins at home.

Did you know?
If all the aluminium cans thrown away in a year were put end to end, they would stand 50 times higher than Mount Everest.

Clean air
Cars use fuel and pump dirty fumes into the air.

Walking to school instead of going by car helps to keep the air clean.

Cycling is a clean form of transport. It does not pollute the air we breathe.

Recycling
Recycling means collecting and then using old materials, such as glass, to make new goods.

1 Used glass bottles are collected at home.

2 Used glass is put into special collection bins.

3 Glass is taken to a recycling factory.

Each bin is for different materials.

Glass is melted down to make new products.

Recycled glass bottles

Clean water
Rubbish and poisons pollute water. This can be dangerous.

People, plants, and animals need clean water to live.

Dirty, polluted water causes illness and infection.

Clean Earth
Chemicals and rubbish pollute the land. They stay in the soil for many years.

Picking up litter keeps the environment clean.

Organic crops are grown without chemicals – keeping the soil clean.

Energy
Burning fuels to make electricity uses up resources.

Recycled glass bulb

Switching off lights saves energy.

Modern wind machines produce electricity without burning fuels.

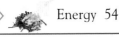
Find out more ▷ Energy 54   Materials 97

Dance

Life Today

Types of dance

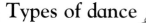

Thai dances are graceful, and were first performed in temples.

Rock and roll dances began in America in the 1950s.

Native American dances all have special meanings.

Country-and-western dance is popular and lots of fun.

Folk dances are the old, traditional dances of a country.

Dancing is moving your body to music. People dance alone, with a partner, or in a group. There are dancing styles around the world.

Spanish flamenco
Flamenco dancing comes from Spain. The dancers stamp and whirl to the music of a guitar.

Long, colourful dresses

Dancers toss their heads.

Flowers worn in hair

Castanets clicked in a rhythm

Did you know?
A limbo dancer once danced under a bar just 15 cm (6 in) off the ground.

Competition dancing

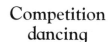

Ballroom dancers are judged on their steps, style, and grace.

Disco dancers are judged on their energy and original movements.

Ballet
Ballet tells stories through dance. It is very old, and there are five basic body positions.

First   Second   Third   Fourth   Fifth

Ballet dancers are strong and fit. They train for many years.

Find out more

 Europe: culture 60

 Music 100

World of Nature

Desert animals

With burning days, freezing nights, and no water, a desert is one of the harshest habitats on Earth. Even so, some animals manage to survive here.

Desert shelter
Like many desert animals, fennec foxes shelter from the Sun in underground burrows.

Desert survival

Harris's hawks build their nests in the prickly branches of a cactus.

Dwarf hamsters have thick fur to help them survive the freezing desert nights.

Darkling wing beetles have white wings to reflect heat, keeping the insects cool.

Bactrian camel
Camels have adapted well to desert life. They can go without water for months.

Thick fur protects the camel from the burning Sun.

Humps store fat for when food is low.

Nostrils can close to keep out sand.

Wide feet stop the camel sinking in the soft sand.

Stomach stores water

Desert reptiles

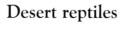
Lizard

Many reptiles live in the desert. Their scaly skin stops them drying out.

Tadpole shrimps can survive under the sand for 10 years, waiting for rain to fall.

Scorpions only hunt in the cool of the night. They kill their prey with a deadly sting.

Did you know?
Male sandgrouse soak up water in their breast feathers and then fly back to their chicks, who drink it all up!

Sand viper

To escape from the Sun, the sand viper buries itself in the sand.

Find out more Africa 6 · · · Deserts 46

World of Nature

Deserts

Desert plants

Kokerboom trees can survive for several years without water.

Barrel cacti store water inside their thick, waxy spines and stems.

Hedgehog cacti grow in rocky deserts and flower when it rains.

Century plants bloom once every 20 to 50 years.

Whisker cactus flowers open at night because most insects feed when it's cool.

Deserts are the driest places on Earth. Instead of soil, the land is covered with bare rock, gravel, or sand, in which very few plants can grow.

Rocky desert
Hot days, freezing nights, and strong winds make desert rocks splinter and crack.

Did you know?
The San people of Africa find tiny wells in the desert. They suck up the water through hollow sticks.

Sandy desert
Strong desert winds blow the sand into ever-changing hills called sand dunes.

Sand dunes can be as tall as a 60-storey building.

An oasis is a place where water flows out of the ground.

Palms and other plants can grow here.

Desert life
People who live in the desert move around, looking for water and grazing land for their animals. They are called nomads.

Bedouin nomads

Saluki dogs are used for hunting.

Arab horses are used for transport.

Many nomads use cloth tents to shelter them from the burning Sun.

Find out more Desert animals 45   South America 130

Life in the Past

Dinosaur types

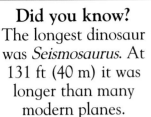

Dinosaurs ruled the Earth for 165 million years. There were over 300 different kinds, but they didn't all live at the same time!

Edmontonia
Edmontonia had spiky body armour. This made it hard to attack.

Duck-like beak

Corythosaurus
Corythosaurus was a duck-billed dinosaur. It lived in the Cretaceous period, and fed on leaves.

Bony crest

Troodon
Troodon used its huge, curved claws to catch its prey.

Oviraptor ate eggs, cracking the shells with its pointed beak.

Stegocerous
used its strong, bony skull to headbutt its enemies.

Compsognathus had a long neck, narrow jaws, and sharp teeth.

Long tail for balance

Strong back legs to run from danger

Front legs pulled down branches.

Euoplocephalus
Leathery skin and spikes protected *Euoplocephalus* from its enemies.

Psittacosaurus
Psittacosaurus used its horny beak to strip plants.

Triceratops had three horns and a frill to protect its neck.

Deinonychus
Deinonychus was a fast and deadly hunter, with strong teeth and sharp claws.

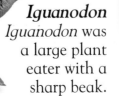

Iguanodon
Iguanodon was a large plant eater with a sharp beak.

Stegosaurus had a small head, with a brain the size of a walnut!

Find out more  Dinosaurs 48   Living things 91

Life in the Past

Dinosaurs

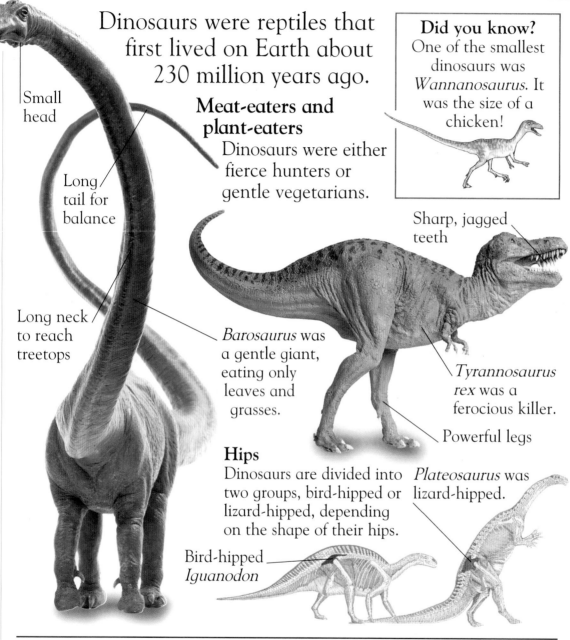

Dinosaurs were reptiles that first lived on Earth about 230 million years ago.

Small head

Long tail for balance

Long neck to reach treetops

Meat-eaters and plant-eaters

Dinosaurs were either fierce hunters or gentle vegetarians.

Barosaurus was a gentle giant, eating only leaves and grasses.

Sharp, jagged teeth

Tyrannosaurus rex was a ferocious killer.

Powerful legs

Hips

Dinosaurs are divided into two groups, bird-hipped or lizard-hipped, depending on the shape of their hips.

Bird-hipped *Iguanodon*

Plateosaurus was lizard-hipped.

Did you know?
One of the smallest dinosaurs was *Wannanosaurus*. It was the size of a chicken!

Changing Earth

The dinosaur age lasted so long that scientists have split it into three parts.

Dinosaurs first appeared 245 million years ago in the **Triassic period**.

In the **Jurassic period**, 208 million years ago, many new dinosaurs appeared.

Dinosaurs died out 65 million years ago at the end of the **Cretaceous period**.

Fossils
Scientists learn about dinosaurs by studying fossils found in the ground.

Struthiomimus

Model of dinosaur nest

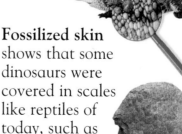

Fossilized bones tell us the shape of these extinct animals.

Fossilized eggs

Crocodile

Fossilized skin shows that some dinosaurs were covered in scales like reptiles of today, such as crocodiles.

Find out more

Dinosaur types 47   Fossils 74

Life in the Past

Early humans

Tools and weapons

Fire sticks

A **stone adze** was used to cut wood or dig up roots.

Diggers were sticks used to dig up grubs from the ground.

A **leather shoulder bag** carried a hunter's bow and arrows.

Arrowheads and blades were made from a hard stone called flint.

Arrows

Fire
Fire kept people warm, cooked their food, and frightened wild animals away.

Dry wood or grass

Clothing
Clothes were made from wool and hairy animal skins.

Wool

Animal skin   Dyes from plants

About 30,000 years ago, people began to shelter in caves, gather their own food, and make tools from wood and stone.

Cave painting
Early artists painted pictures of animals on cave walls.

Rubbing sticks together made a spark. This set fire to the grass.

Bread made from grains

Nuts and berries

Food
People hunted animals, dug up roots, and gathered seeds for food.

Salmon

Deer

Bronze age
Bronze was first used about 5,000 years ago to make metal objects.

Sickle to cut crops

Neck ring

Pin

Belt decoration

Iron age
Iron is a harder metal than bronze. It was first made about 4,000 years ago.

Bracelet

Razor

Brooch

Dagger

Did you know?
Early humans met and knew only about 25 people in their entire lifetime!

Find out more 〉 Fossils 74   Materials 97

Science and Technology

Earth

The atmosphere
The atmosphere is made up of several different layers.

The highest layer is 430 miles (700 km) above the Earth. Satellites fly here.

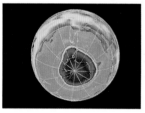

The ozone layer
contains ozone gas, which protects Earth from the Sun's rays.

The middle layer is up to 30 miles (50 km) high. Planes fly here, above the clouds.

The lowest layer is only 7 miles (10 km) high. It contains the gases we need to live.

The Earth is a giant rocky ball spinning in space. It is surrounded by the atmosphere – layers of air that protect the planet and provide the oxygen we need to breathe.

Inside the Earth
The Earth is made up of different layers of rock and metal.

The inner core is a ball of hot, solid metal.

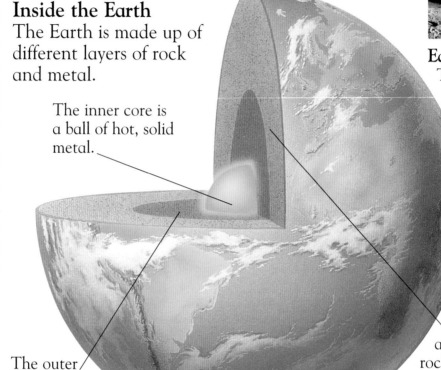

The outer core is a very thick liquid metal.

Earth from space
This picture of Earth was taken by a camera on board a spacecraft.

The crust is the rocky layer on which we live.

The mantle is a thick layer of rock. It is very hot and some of it moves like treacle.

Earth's ingredients
The **crust** is made up of basalt and granite.

The **mantle** is a mix of metals like peridotite.

The **core** is made of solid metals like iron.

Basalt   Granite

Peridotite

Iron

Did you know?
The Earth's crust, when compared to the whole of the Earth, is thinner than the skin of an apple.

Water and ice cover over three-quarters of the Earth's surface.

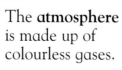

The **atmosphere** is made up of colourless gases.

Find out more Planets 109   Rocks and minerals 120

World of Nature

Eggs and nests

Types of egg

Butterfly eggs are laid on leaves and look like tiny jewels.

Frogs lay hundreds of eggs in water, protected by jelly.

Tortoise eggs are soft and leathery and buried in sand.

Hens' eggs are soft at first, but harden quickly as they dry.

Dogfish lay their tough egg cases among seaweed.

Slugs lay clear eggs in damp places, like a log pile.

Birds and insects, frogs and snakes – most animals lay eggs. But some animals build nests especially to protect their eggs and babies.

Bird's nest
Birds collect all sorts of materials to make a warm, comfortable home, like this wagtail's nest.

Moss for warmth

Did you know ?
Red-billed hornbills make nests in hollow trees, sealing off the entrance until their chicks hatch.

Feathers for warmth

String

Twigs for structure

Shiny foil

Lichen for camouflage

Mud mixed with spit

Horse hair

Unusual nests

Male **weaver birds** use their beaks and claws to weave wonderful nests of grass.

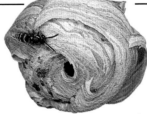

Wasp nests are made from chewed-up wood and feel like paper.

Quails scrape out nests among rocks and dirt, which help to hide their brown, speckled eggs.

Electricity

Electricity is a kind of energy. It is useful because it can be made easily, and sent into homes, where it provides heat, light, and power.

Did you know?
One flash of lightning has the same power as 50 million batteries!

Coal

Fuel
Coal, oil, and gas are all used in power stations.

Oil

Gas

Coal-fired power station
This power station burns coal to heat water and make steam. The steam turns turbines which produce electricity.

Coal burns in a furnace.

Steam escapes through chimneys.

Types of energy
Electricity can be produced in a variety of ways.

Hydro-electric dams use the power of running water to make electricity.

Solar power uses the Sun's light rays to produce electricity.

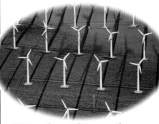

Wind turbines have huge sails that turn in the wind helping to make electricity.

Pylon
From the power station electricity is transported along wire cables supported by pylons.

Electricity cable
In towns, most cables are buried underground, a few are carried on small poles.

Nuclear power stations use chemical reactions to make electricity.

Lightning
Lightning is a kind of electricity. It is as natural as wind and rain.

Battery power
Batteries contain chemicals that make electricity. Batteries are used to power things like toys and torches.

Battery

Battery-run car

Find out more ▶ Electricity at home 53   Oil 106

Electricity at home

In the kitchen

Ovens
often use electricity to heat up and cook our food.

Microwaves run on electricity. They cook food very quickly.

Fridges use electricity to keep food cool and fresh.

It's hard to imagine life without electricity. We use it to heat and light our homes, cook our food, listen to music, and talk on the phone.

Light
Electric lighting is bright and safe. It replaced candles and gas lamps, used in the past.

Lamp

Light bulb
Electricity makes light bulbs glow and give out light.

At night, lights shine out in the dark.

Electric plug
Electricity flows along wires, and into the plugs in the wall sockets.

Safety in the home
Electricity can be very dangerous.

Never touch damaged wires.

Never use electrical objects near water.

Entertainment

Televisions use electricity to make sounds and pictures.

Computers are powerful machines. They use very little electricity.

Telephones use electricity to change our voices into signals.

Energy

A person running, a fire burning, a plant growing – all these things use energy. Energy makes things happen. Without it, there would be no life on Earth.

Sun
The Sun provides the energy all living things need.

People and energy
Your body needs energy for everything you do – whether you're thinking, working, or running.

Runners use up huge amounts of energy.

Athletes eat high-energy food.

Food for energy
People and animals get energy from the food they eat. Some foods give us more energy than others.

Calories
The energy value of food is measured in calories. Pasta has more calories and gives us more energy than carrots.

Pasta

Carrot

Types of energy
Energy comes in many forms.

Heat energy can be used to cook food and keep us warm.

Light energy can come from a flame, electric light or the Sun.

Sound energy is produced when something vibrates.

Chemical energy is stored in plants. Animals eat the plants and use the energy.

Electrical energy is the main source of power in modern homes.

Did you know?
Old animal droppings can be a source of energy. They give off a gas that burns.

Machines
All machines need energy to work. A car gets energy from burning petrol, but a bike gets its energy from you!

Energy supplies

Oil

Gas   Coal

Oil, coal, and gas are all sources of energy. But these fuels will run out one day.

Find out more Food and eating 70   Oil 106

Continents of the World

Europe

Central Europe

The area of Central Europe covers many countries. It is is a region of flat farmland, wooded hills, and snow-capped mountains.

Did you know?
- Wild pigs called boars still live in the forests of central Europe.
- The River Rhine is 1,320 km (820 miles) long – the length of the UK.

River Rhine
The Rhine is an important riverway for transporting cargo across the region.

Netherlands
The low-lying land by the sea is flat and fertile – perfect for growing bulbs.

European bison
Bison once lived in huge herds. Now they are protected.

Map

NETHERLANDS
AMSTERDAM
River Lek
BELGIUM
BRUSSELS
ARDENNES
River Rhine
LUXEMBOURG

Capital cities
1 LUXEMBOURG
2 VADUZ

River Elbe
BERLIN
GERMANY
BLACK FOREST
River Danube

P O L A N D
WARSAW
River Odra

PRAGUE
CZECH REPUBLIC

River Vistula
CARPATHIAN MOUNTAINS
SLOVAKIA

VIENNA
BRATISLAVA
River Danube
BUDAPEST

A L P S
BERN
SWITZERLAND
Mount Eiger
LIECHTENSTEIN
N

AUSTRIA
HUNGARY

Carpathian Mountains
These mountains lie to the east of Europe.

Mount Eiger
Mount Eiger is one of the highest peaks in the Alps.

The Ardennes
This is an area of hills and valleys in southern Belgium.

Black Forest
The Black Forest in Germany is an area of wooded mountains.

River Danube
This river runs through six countries in central Europe.

Find out more 🐐 Mammals of the world 95 | Rivers and lakes 119

Continents of the World

Europe: culture

Central Europe

Central Europe has a very large population. Many of the people live in busy and crowded cities.

Winter sports
Many people go to the Austrian and Swiss Alps to enjoy the winter sports.

Skiing

Prague
The capital of the Czech Republic has some of the most beautiful architecture in Europe.

Opera house

The Old Town Bridge Tower

River Vltava

Regional food

Root vegetables, such as potatoes and turnips are grown in Poland.

Mussels and chips are a popular dish. They are often eaten in Belgium.

Swiss chocolate is made with the milk from Switzerland's famous dairy herds.

Edam cheese is traditionally made in the Netherlands.

Pretzels are made from wheat. They are popular in Germany.

Industry
Germany manufactures cars for countries all over the world.

Regional products

Cuckoo clocks and watches are made in Switzerland.

Tulips
Tulips are flown all around the world from the Netherlands.

National costume
Poland's national costume is worn for celebrations.

Architecture
The architecture of central Europe is highly decorative, such as this church in Vienna.

Find out more Sports of the world 136   Towns and cities 140

Continents of the World

Europe

Northern Europe
This cool, wet region has snowy mountains and pine forests in the north, and rolling hills in the south.

Pine forest
The tough northern pine forests survive the bitterly cold winters.

Hot springs
In Iceland, hot springs, called geysers, spurt out of the ground.

Fjord
Norway's fjords are deep inlets carved into the coastline by rivers of ice.

ICELAND
• REYKJAVIK

Cotswolds
The English landscape has many gently rolling hills, but no high mountains.

Scottish highlands
Scotland is a land of rugged mountains and beautiful lakes.

Rhododendron
This evergreen plant survives cold winters. It lives throughout northern Europe.

HIGHLANDS
SCOTLAND

NORTHERN IRELAND

REPUBLIC OF IRELAND
DUBLIN •

UNITED KINGDOM

WALES   ENGLAND
COTSWOLDS
LONDON •

N

Lake Inari

F I N L A N D

Lake Oulu

N O R W A Y

S W E D E N

HELSINKI •

• TALLINN

ESTONIA

OSLO •

STOCKHOLM •

Lake Vänern

RIGA

LATVIA

LITHUANIA

VILNIUS •

COPENHAGEN •
DENMARK

Midnight Sun
In the far north, the midsummer Sun never sets. There is daylight even at night!

Did you know?
• In Iceland there is so much hot water under the ground, that it is used to heat whole towns.
• There are over 100,000 lakes in Sweden.

Red squirrel
Red squirrels live in forests, feeding on nuts and seeds.

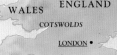

Find out more Climates 39   Forests 73

Europe: culture

Northern Europe
The industrial countries of Northern Europe still have strong traditions of farming and fishing.

Did you know?
In Denmark there are twice as many pigs as people!

Tea
The British are famous for drinking tea.

London
London is the capital of the United Kingdom. It is a modern city with many historical buildings.

Big Ben clock tower

Houses of Parliament

London bus

Regional products

Cheese   Butter

Dairy products are widespread in northern Europe, especially in Ireland.

Lego is a world-famous toy from Denmark.

Timber from the region's forests is sold around the world.

Aircraft, such as this Concorde, are produced all over the United Kingdom.

Rugby
Rugby is a popular sport throughout the United Kingdom.

Fishing
Many of the countries in this region have large fishing fleets.

Culture

Tartan is a traditional Scottish material.

Wooden stave churches were once built in Norway.

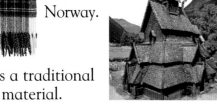

Smörgasbord is a cold buffet, served in Sweden.

Sami
The Sami people live a traditional life, herding reindeer in Lapland.

Find out more ➤ Fish of the world 68   Sport 135

Continents of the World

Europe

Southern Europe

Southern Europe stretches down to the Mediterranean Sea. It is a dry, hilly land, with hot summers and mild winters.

Did you know?
- Huge flocks of flamingoes fly to southern Europe in the summer months.
- There are 36 villages built on the slopes of the active volcano, Mount Etna.

Provence
Wild herbs grow in the hills of Provence in southern France.

Alps
The Alps are the longest and highest mountain range in Europe.

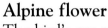

Alpine flower
The bird's-eye primrose flowers in early summer.

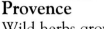

N

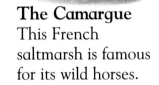

The Camargue
This French saltmarsh is famous for its wild horses.

Meseta Plain
The Meseta Plain lies in the middle of Spain. It is a high, rocky area with very few trees.

Rock of Gibraltar
This rocky cliff lies at the tip of Spain. It is home to the only monkeys in Europe.

Mount Etna
Mount Etna is an active volcano on the island of Sicily. It last erupted in 1995.

Greek islands
Greece is a hot, dry land with hundreds of small islands in a warm, blue sea.

Olive tree
Olive trees grow on the dry southern hills.

Find out more ▷ Flowers 69 Mountains 99

Continents of the World

Europe: culture

Southern Europe

These countries are rich in history, and are world-famous for their good food and wonderful wines.

Did you know?
The Vatican City is the smallest state in the world.

Vatican City, Rome
The Vatican City, in Rome, is the headquarters of the Catholic Church.

Industry
Wine is made from grapes throughout this region.

Cork is made from the bark of the cork oak tree, which grows in Portugal.

Grand Piazza   St Peter's Basilica

Beaches on the Mediterranean coast attract many tourists to southern Europe.

Tourism
Ancient ruins, such as the temple of Apollo in Greece, are popular with tourists.

Fishing
Fishing is very important in Greece. The seas contain squid, sardines, and tunny fish.

Architecture

Châteaux are old castles that were built in France about 400 years ago.

Orthodox churches in Greece are richly decorated on the inside.

Greek houses have white walls to reflect the heat of the Sun in summer.

Ancient buildings, like this tower, are found in Portugal.

Food
Southern Europe has many famous foods and dishes that are eaten worldwide.

  Olive oil   Oranges   Paella   Cheese   Lamb kebabs   Pasta

Find out more Foods of the world 71   Homes and houses 78

Life in the Past

Explorers

Travellers

Pacific Islanders were the first to cross the Pacific Ocean.

The **Vikings** sailed to the south to find fertile farmland.

Viking helmet

Merchants explored the route between China and Europe to trade in silk.

Arabs travelled in the 13th century to trade and find new lands.

Astrolabe

Columbus, a Spanish explorer, crossed the Atlantic Ocean using an astrolabe.

For thousands of years people have explored the world, hoping to find fertile farmland, fine goods, and riches.

Round Earth
In 1519 a famous Spanish explorer, Magellan, sailed around the world – and proved it was round.

Four masts for large sails

Ship's compass

Sailing ship
Starting in the 1400s, European sailors explored the world in fast, sturdy ships like this one.

Sailors spotted land from the crow's nest.

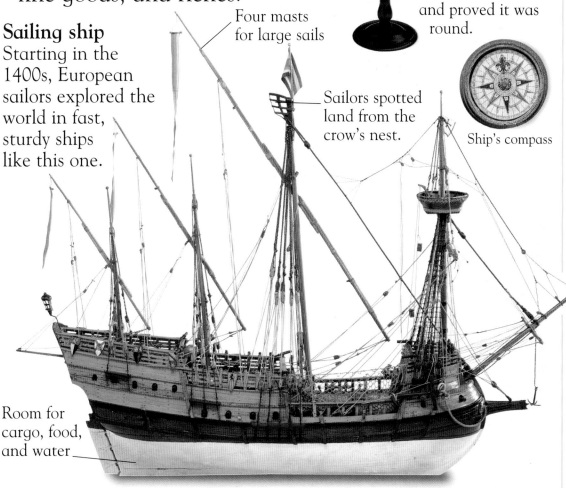

Room for cargo, food, and water

Finding the way
Explorers used the Sun, stars, and instruments to find their way.

Sextant

Backstaff

Telescope

Goods
Explorers brought home new foods and riches from around the world.

Jade

Cloves

Cinnamon

Pineapple

Did you know?
Before the 1520s, most people thought the world was flat!

Find out more

 Vikings 145

Ships and boats 127

Science and Technology

Factories

Chocolate factory

A chocolate factory is organized so that chocolate bars can be made quickly and cheaply.

Clothes, chocolate, cars – almost everything we buy is mass produced in factories. Factories use machines to make goods in their thousands.

1 Raw materials
All the chocolate ingredients are sent to the factory.

Sugar   Milk   Cocoa pods

2 Production process
Machines make the chocolate, pour it into moulds, and wrap it when it's cold and hard.

Chocolate bars on conveyor belt

Chocolate checked for quality.

3 Finished product
The finished chocolate bars are packed and taken to the shops, ready for you to buy.

Chocolate bar

Leather goods
This shoe factory uses the leftover shoe leather to make other goods, such as wallets and key rings.

Types of factory

A **hat factory** makes thousands of hats of one style at a time.

Washing machine factories test all the machines before they leave.

Computer factories assemble hundreds of new computers on a conveyor belt.

Car factories use robots to put cars together.

Food factories keep their machines very clean so that the food is safe to eat.

Find out more ➤  Computers 42 South America: culture 132

Life Today

Farm animals

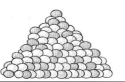
Farmers have kept and reared animals for thousands of years. They provide people with food and other useful materials.

Types of farm animal

Llamas provide milk, meat, leather, and wool.

Sheep
Farmers around the world keep sheep for their meat, milk, and soft, warm wool. The sheep are kept in flocks.

Warm coat in winter

Sheep shearing

Types of cattle farming

Hereford bull

Some cattle are farmed for meat.

Jersey cow

Others are farmed for their milk.

Sheep's milk

Wool is used to make clothing, fabrics, and carpets.

Wool comes off in one piece called a fleece.

Sheep's cheese

Turkeys are bred for their meat.

Ostriches are farmed for their skin, meat, and feathers.

Pigs are farmed for their meat and leather.

Fish farming

Short coat keeps sheep cool in summer.

Sheep's wool is warm and greasy.

Trout and salmon are reared on fish farms. The farms provide cheap fish.

Free-range farming
Free-range farming allows farm animals to wander around freely.

Intensive farming
Some farmers keep animals indoors in small pens. This is called intensive farming.

Find out more Australasia: culture 28   Farming 64

Farming

Life Today

Most of the food that we buy every day in the shops is grown on farms throughout the world.

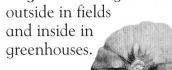

In some countries, farmers use rice harvesters to gather rice quickly.

Rice plants grow in water.

More than half the world's people live on rice.

Flooded rice fields are called paddy fields.

Rice farming
Most rice is grown in parts of Asia, where the weather is warm and wet.

Most of the work is done by hand.

Did you know?
In southern Europe, farmers use pigs to find mushrooms called truffles.

Rice products

Fried rice

Rice cakes   Noodles

Rice paper

Farm tools and machines

Ox-drawn ploughs slowly break up the soil for planting.

Tractors are expensive, but powerful. This one is sowing seeds.

Crop sprayers spray chemicals over plants to protect them from pests.

Pitchforks are an old farm tool. They are used to pick up hay.

Scythes are used to harvest crops by hand. The blade is very sharp.

Combine harvesters gather cereal crops quickly and efficiently.

Farm crops
Vegetables are grown outside in fields and inside in greenhouses.

Squash

Sugar beet

Fruits grow on plantations, in orchards, and fields.

Cape gooseberry

Apples

Maize

Cereals, such as wheat and maize, grow in huge fields around the world.

Wheat

Find out more ⟩ Asia: culture 21   Foods of the world 71

Festivals

Festivals are special days in the year when people celebrate and remember events in the past.

March to May

In **Holy week** Christians remember when Jesus died and then rose again.

Mardi Gras

Mardi Gras is a festival in Brazil. Christians used to celebrate this day before beginning a 40-day fast.

June to August

The **summer solstice** has been celebrated for 4,000 years. People gather to watch the sun rise on Midsummer's Day.

September to November

Halloween was once a time to scare away evil spirits. Today it is a day of fun.

On **Thanksgiving Day** American families eat together and give thanks for the harvest.

Colourful costumes

Dancing crowds

December to February

At **Chinese New Year** a dragon dances through the streets, chasing away the past.

At **Christmas**, Christians remember the birth of Jesus and give presents.

Festival customs

Candles are a symbol of life and truth.

Costumes often have special meaning. They may be a disguise.

Music helps people to have fun together.

Dances are a way of re-living customs of the past.

Did you know?
On March 1st, Greeks smash jugs against their front doors to get rid of mice and fleas.

Find out more ▷ Ancient China 12   Religions 115

Life Today

Film

Did you know?
The first films had no sound. Someone played the piano while the film ran.

Films tell stories using moving pictures, sound, and special effects. They are great entertainment.

Clapper board

Microphones pick up every sound.

Film set
It takes a large team of people, and a lot of money, to make a film.

Camera

Film history

Silent films were the first films. They were in black and white.

Engineers control the lighting.

The director is in charge.

Actors

Talkies appeared in 1927. People flocked to the cinema to hear actors speak.

Colour films were a hit when they arrived in the 1930s.

Types of films
Millions of people go to the cinema to see many different types of film.

Science fiction

Western

Horror

Special effect films use the latest computer technology.

Cartoon
Cartoon films are made up of many drawings, which move when run together.

Find out more Asia: culture 25 Computers 42

World of Nature

Fish

Fish live in the world's rivers, lakes, and seas. The way fish look, move, and breathe is perfectly suited to their underwater life.

Did you know?
Male catfish carry the females' eggs inside their mouths until they hatch.

Fins help fish to steer.

Goldfish
A fish's body is smooth and streamlined, just like this goldfish. It is the perfect shape for moving quickly through water.

Tail fin works like a paddle.

Gills

Eye

Scaly skin

Fin

Types of fish

Bony fish, such as mackerel, is the largest group of fish.

Jawless fish is a small group and includes lampreys.

Sharks, such as the leopard shark, have their own group.

Breathing
Fish breathe underwater with their gills. These take oxygen from the water as the fish swims along.

Eggs
Most fish lay millions of jelly-like eggs straight into the sea. This is called spawning.

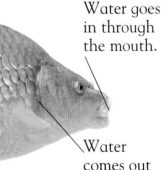

Water goes in through the mouth.

Water comes out of the gills.

Defence

A shoal of dart fish is harder to attack than one fish on its own.

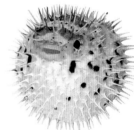

Long spines make the pufferfish almost impossible to swallow!

Camouflage helps flounders to blend in with the sea bed.

Torpedo rays give an electric shock when they are attacked.

Find out more ⟩ Fish of the world 68   Sea animals 123

Fish of the world

There are over 30,000 different kinds of fish in the world today. Just over half of them live in salty seawater. The others live in freshwater lakes, rivers, and streams.

Stickleback
Sticklebacks live in the Atlantic Ocean. They feed on smaller fish.

Leopard shark
This harmless shark lives and hunts in the Pacific Ocean.

Tiger barb
This tiny, stripy fish lives in streams and rivers on warm Pacific islands.

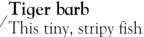

European eel
These eels live in the rivers of Europe but travel far out into the ocean to breed.

ARCTIC OCEAN

EUROPE

NORTH AMERICA

ASIA

ATLANTIC OCEAN

AFRICA

PACIFIC OCEAN

SOUTH AMERICA

INDIAN OCEAN

AUSTRALASIA

ANTARCTICA

Piranha
Piranhas are deadly hunters. They live in the rivers of the South American rainforest.

Queen angelfish
This tropical fish lives in the coral reefs of the Pacific Ocean. Its colouring helps it to hide in the coral.

Where fish live

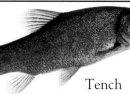
Tench

Seas and oceans
Many saltwater fish live near the surface, some swim in shoals deeper down, while others lie on the sea bed itself.

Butterflyfish

Ocean deep
Only a few fish can survive in the cold, dark water in the deepest parts of the ocean.

Rivers and lakes
Freshwater fish are often more colourful than the fish of the sea. Different kinds choose to live in still or fast-flowing water.

Angler fish

Tropical seas
The warm, shallow tropical seas are home to some of the world's most beautiful fish.

Cod

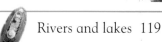

Find out more ▸ 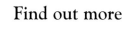 Fish 67   Rivers and lakes 119

World of Nature

Flowers

We love flowers for their colour, shape, and scent. Yet their loveliness is not for us; it's to attract small creatures to visit them.

Did you know?
The Venus flytrap gets extra food by trapping and digesting small insects!

Lily
Flowers can look very different from each other, but they all have the same basic parts – just like this lily.

Rose

Perfume
Many flowers have a sweet smell and are used to make soaps, oils, and perfumes.

Petal
Petals come in many shapes, sizes, and colours to attract insects and birds, which pollinate the flowers.

Petal

Patterns lead insects into the centre.

The sticky stigma collects pollen from other lily plants.

Stamens make a fine yellow dust called pollen.

Pollination
Pollen must be carried from one flower to another to make seeds.

1 A bee visits a flower to feed on its sweet nectar.

2 As the bee feeds, pollen on the stamens sticks to its legs.

3 At the next flower, the pollen brushes on to the stigma.

4 This flower is now pollinated, and can begin to make seeds.

Unusual flowers

Water Lily flowers float on water.

Grasses have dull flowers.

Urn plants have red flowers to attract birds.

Catkins are groups of tiny flowers found on some trees.

Find out more Fruits and seeds 75   Plants 110

Science and Technology

Food and eating

Did you know?
A person eats about 30 tonnes (33 tons) of food in a lifetime – the same weight as six African elephants.

A good diet
The food you eat is called your diet. A healthy diet has food from five different groups. Each group helps your body in a different way.

Proteins help the body grow and repair itself. They are found in meat, fish, dairy products, and nuts.

To keep strong and healthy, it is important to eat the right foods. Food gives us energy as well as being a pleasure to eat!

Vitamins and minerals in fresh fruit and vegetables help fight disease.

Fat is found in oil, butter, and avocados, and is stored in the body for extra energy.

Preserving food

Dried foods, such as beans and herbs, have all their water removed.

Pickled foods, such as fruit and vegetables, are preserved in vinegar or a sugary syrup.

Canned foods, like fruit, fish, and meat, are packed in liquid in a sealed can.

Frozen foods, such as meat, fish, and vegetables, keep well for several months.

Smoked foods, such as fish and bacon, are dried, or cured, in a room full of smoke.

Digestion
1 From your mouth, food goes to your stomach.

2 Your stomach juices turn the food into liquid.

3 The liquid is squeezed along the intestines. Here the goodness passes into your blood.

4 The leftovers are pushed out when you go to the toilet.

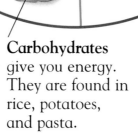

Carbohydrates give you energy. They are found in rice, potatoes, and pasta.

Water
Your body needs about 3 litres (5 pints) of water every day.

Fibre helps food move through your intestines. Cereals, nuts, beans, and bread all contain fibre.

70

Find out more 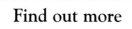 Farming 64 Foods of the world 71

Foods of the world

Pineapples, peanuts, and pears –
our food comes from all over the
world, adding colour, flavour,
and goodness to our diet.

Did you know?
Every day humans
eat a pile of rice over
six times bigger than
the Great Pyramid
in Egypt!

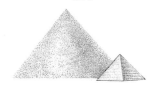

Olive oil
Olives grow in the
hot, dry climate of
southern Europe. The
olives are squeezed
to make oil.

Root vegetables
Root vegetables, such
as turnips, grow well in
the cool, wet
climate of
northern Asia.

Wheat
Canada has the
ideal climate for
wheat. It needs a
wet spring and a
dry summer.

Bananas
Bananas grow in
a hot, tropical
climate, like
that of South
America.

Chocolate
Chocolate is
made from the
beans of the cacao
tree. These grow in the
hot, wet African rainforests.

Peaches
Peaches are grown
in Australia,
where there are
cool springs and
hot summers.

Tea
Tea plants grow in
warm, wet, and hilly
areas throughout
southeast Asia.

Transporting food

Planes are used
to transport
fruit and
vegetables.
Fresh food,
like oranges,
rots if it is
not eaten
quickly.

Orange grove

Fishing boats, far from
land, pack the fish they
catch in ice. This keeps
the fish fresh until the
boat is brought to shore.

Trucks carry dried foods,
like spices, to a market.
Dried foods
keep well.

Find out more ▸ Asia: culture 25 · Food and eating 70

World of Nature

Forest animals

Forests make a wonderful home for animals. The trees provide them with everything they need – food, hiding places, and shelter from the cold.

Forest minibeasts

Squirrel
Squirrels feed on nuts, cones, and insects.

Earthworms drag dead leaves under the soil, which makes it more fertile.

Forest birds

Woodpeckers drill holes into trees to make nests and eat insects under the bark.

Badger
Badgers live in underground burrows. They hunt at night.

Powerful jaws to tear out tough roots

Wood ants live in colonies of up to 100,000 ants. They eat other insects.

Crossbills have twisted beaks, which they use to open cones.

Raccoon
Raccoons climb trees to steal eggs from nests.

Grizzly bear
Bears feed on plants, tree roots, and small animals. They are well adapted to forest life.

Millipedes scurry through the leaves on the forest floor.

Jays feed on seeds, but they also steal eggs from other birds' nests.

Thick fur to keep warm

Weevils help to break down dead plants.

Strong claws to dig out roots and grip trees

Strong legs for climbing trees

Centipedes live in the soil, catching small animals with their special claws.

Tawny owls spend all day hiding in a tree, then come out to hunt at night.

Find out more   Animals in danger 18   Forests 73

World of Nature

Forests

Forests grow in many different parts of the world. There are three main types of forest: coniferous, deciduous, and rainforest.

Deciduous forest

A deciduous forest contains a mix of different trees. Most of them lose their leaves in the autumn, and grow new ones in the spring.

Horse chestnut leaf

Autumn leaf colour

Trees are a rounded shape.

Variety of trees

Deciduous forest plants

Mushrooms rot down dead plants, keeping the soil fertile for plants.

Primroses bloom in the spring, before the leaves on the trees block out the Sun.

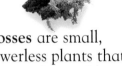

Mosses are small, flowerless plants that grow in damp places.

Oak leaf in autumn

Maple leaf in autumn

Leaves
The broad, flat leaves change colour in the autumn.

Oak leaf

Mountain ash blossom

Blossom
Trees grow flowers to attract insects.

Seeds
Seeds often grow inside a tasty fruit.

Rowan tree berries

Bluebells cover the forest floor with a carpet of purple flowers.

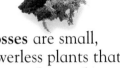
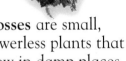

Coniferous forest

Coniferous forests contain evergreen trees, which can survive very cold weather. Evergreens shed some needles all year round.

Snow slides off the branches.

Trees are a triangular shape.

Leaves
Leaves, called needles, are thin and tough.

Pine needles

Spruce cones

Pine cones

Poor, infertile soil

Cones
Seeds are protected inside a cone.

Did you know?
If polluted air mixes with rain, it can make acid rain. This harms forests by damaging leaves on trees.

Find out more ➤ Rainforests 114   Trees 143

Fossils

Fossils are the remains of plants and animals that lived millions of years ago. When discovered, they give us fascinating clues to the past.

Plant fossils

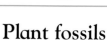

This **poplar leaf** fossil looks like poplar leaves today.

Mammoth
This huge mammal is now extinct. It was found frozen in the soil.

Shark's tooth
A tooth can tell scientists the size of an extinct animal.

Dung
This dropping came from a shark-like animal.

Fin

Eye socket

Ammonite

Ammonites were sea creatures that are now extinct.

Print of skeleton

Outline of soft tissue in rock

These **seed** fossils are about 30 million years old.

Bark fossils tell us which plants were growing millions of years ago.

Ichthyosaur
This fossil of an extinct sea reptile was formed when the earth around the ichthyosaur turned into stone.

Early human skull
This fossilized skull teaches scientists about the first humans.

Dinosaur footprint
This fossilized footprint shows how big and heavy the dinosaur was.

Amber spider
This spider has been fossilized in amber, the juice of an ancient plant.

Did you know?
This man died 1,740 years ago, but his body was preserved in a peat bog in Denmark.

Fossil hunting
Only the simplest tools are needed to find fossils.

Fossils are very fragile. They must be uncovered very carefully.

A magnifying glass is useful to examine a fossil.

Find out more ▸ Dinosaurs 48   Rocks and minerals 120

World of Nature

Fruits and seeds

Different seeds
Seeds come in all shapes and sizes. They are protected in many different ways.

We think of fruits as juicy foods, like peaches and grapes. But fruits are really seed cases, and they certainly can't all be eaten!

Making seeds

1 As soon as a flower is pollinated, it starts to grow seeds.

Acorns are the fruit of the oak tree. Fruits that have hard, woody shells, are called nuts.

Peas are seeds. They grow inside a fruit called a peapod.

Dates are the fruits of palm trees. Each date contains one seed.

2 The petals drop off, leaving just a seed case.

Sycamore
seeds grow inside a seed case that is wing-shaped.

Lemon seeds are called pips. They are protected by a fruit with juicy flesh and a tough skin.

3 As the seeds grow, the seed case grows bigger, too. This is the fruit.

Prickly pear seeds grow inside a thick, spiky-skinned fruit.

Spreading seeds
Seeds need to move away from their parent plant so that they will have plenty of room to grow.

Walkers carry seeds around in the mud on their boots.

4 The fruit ripens at the same time as the seeds inside.

Dandelion seeds float through the air on fluffy parachutes.

Did you know?
The world's largest seed is from the coco de la mer palm tree. It can weigh as much as 20 kg (44 lb).

Prickly burrs stick to animals' coats and are carried away.

Berries are eaten by birds, which leave the seeds in their droppings.

Coconuts float out to sea and are washed up on other beaches.

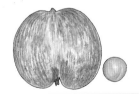

Find out more Flowers 69   Plants 110

World of Nature

Grassland animals

Burrowing animals

Meerkats live in Africa in large groups under the ground.

Wild **guinea pigs** are found in South America. They live in the old burrows of other animals.

Wild **hamsters** live in Russia. To stay safe, they only leave their burrows at night.

Dingos are wild dogs which come from Australia. They live in other animals' burrows.

Many grassland animals have their food right under their feet! But life can be dangerous because there is nowhere to hide from predators.

Savanna animals
The savanna grasslands of Africa are home to huge herds of animals. They roam together looking for food and water.

Giraffes eat leaves off the scattered trees.

Wildebeest move around in huge herds. They are safer that way.

Did you know?
The fastest human runs 100 m (329 ft) in just under 10 seconds. But the cheetah can run it in 3.6 seconds!

Rhea
Rheas live in South America. They can't fly, but can run very fast from their enemies.

Echidna
Echidnas live in the Australian grasslands. In danger, they roll up, showing only their spikes.

Serval
Servals are wild cats that live in Africa. They run very fast and have excellent hearing.

Wallaby
Wallabies live and feed in the Australian grasslands. They can move very fast when in danger.

Secretary bird
Secretary birds have such long legs that they can walk through tall grasses. They live in Africa.

Find out more

Africa 6   Grasslands 77

World of Nature

Grasslands

Grasslands are vast, flat, grassy plains. Few trees grow there because it is too dry. Grasslands have different names around the world.

Prairies
The prairies lie in the centre of North America. The fertile land has been turned into wheat fields.

Small scrub tree

Flat, dry land

Savanna
The tropical grasslands of Africa are called the savanna. The weather is warm, but very little rain falls.

Grasses grazed by herds of animals

Grasses
There are many kinds of grasses. But they are all very adaptable.

Grasses can dry out or even burn, but will grow back within hours of rain.

Pampas grasses have strong woody stems to keep them upright in strong wind.

Cereals are grasses grown on the prairies. They include maize and wheat, and are resistant to disease.

Pampas
The pampas of South America are used for cattle ranching. Cowboys on the pampas are called gauchos.

Gaucho

Mongolian nomad

Nomadic tent

Steppe
Steppe land exists across Asia. These cold, but fertile plains are home to nomads, who move with their animals in search of grazing land.

Did you know?
Bamboo is the fastest growing grass in the world. It can grow 1 m (3 ft) a day – the same height as a 2-year-old child.

Outback
In the dry Australian outback there are huge sheep farms called stations.

Find out more ➤ Australasia 26   Grassland animals 76

Life Today

Homes and houses

Family house
Homes are often made of local materials suitable for the weather.

Home is where you live, eat, and sleep together as a family or alone. Homes give shelter from the weather.

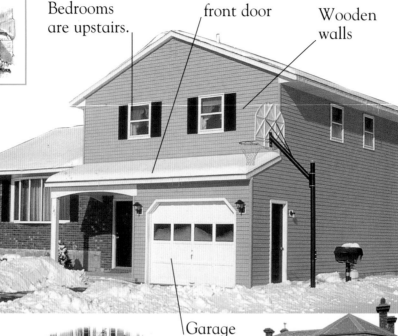

Bedrooms are upstairs.

Porch over front door

Wooden walls

Garage

Homes of the world

Swiss mountain chalets have sloping roofs to shed snow.

Greek homes often have white walls to reflect the Sun's heat.

New Guinea homes are built over lakes on stilts.

Nigerian homes are sometimes made of mud and straw.

Tunisian homes can be built underground to keep them cool.

Tower block
Tower blocks contain flats for lots of people.

Apartment blocks
Apartments lie near the centre of many cities.

Bungalow
Bungalows have no stairs. They are built on one level.

Moving homes
Some people live in homes that can be moved around.

Tepees and other tents are quick and easy to put up.

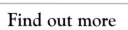

Campers are comfortable homes on wheels.

Houseboats are floating homes on a river or canal.

Caravans are homes pulled by horses or vehicles.

Find out more

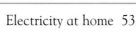 Electricity at home 53

 Towns and cities 140

Life Today

Hospitals and doctors

Hospitals are places where doctors and nurses care for people when they are sick or injured.

Accidents and emergencies
After an accident, patients are taken to the casualty department. Doctors examine them when they arrive.

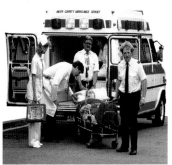

1 Ambulances take emergency patients to hospital very quickly.

2 X-rays show whether the patient has broken any bones.

Did you know?
In some countries, mobile hospitals visit patients – instead of the other way round.

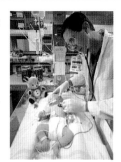

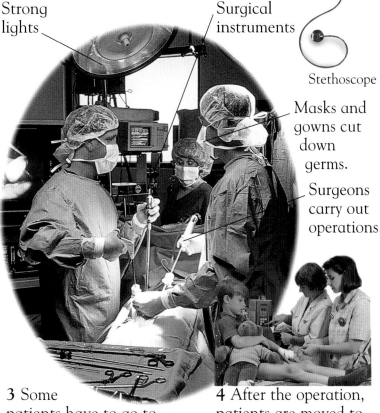

Strong lights

Surgical instruments

Stethoscope

Masks and gowns cut down germs.

Surgeons carry out operations.

3 Some patients have to go to an operating theatre for an operation.

4 After the operation, patients are moved to a ward to rest and recover their strength.

Doctors at work

Local doctors often treat patients at their surgery.

Doctors sometimes treat people at the scene of an accident.

Doctors give some people a health check-up at work.

Doctors visit their most poorly patients in the home.

Some doctors have to fly to patients who live far away.

Intensive care
Very sick patients may need special equipment to stay alive. This is called intensive care.

Nurses
Nurses care for patients both in hospitals and at home.

District nurse

Hospital nurse

Find out more ▷ Human body: skeleton 82   Trucks 144

Science and Technology

Human body: growth

From the moment our lives begin, our bodies are always changing. Our minds grow, too, as we learn more about the world around us.

Did you know?

At the age of two years, a boy is half his adult height!

Starting life

An **embryo** is a group of cells that grows into a baby inside its mother.

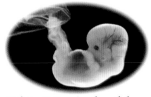

This **10-week-old foetus** has grown from the embryo.

This **five-month-old foetus** looks like a tiny human.

A **newborn baby** sucks milk from its mother.

Growing up

It takes about eighteen years to become a fully grown adult.

Young teenager
Fully grown adult
Baby
Elderly adult
Child

Boys and girls

Boys' and girls' bodies and minds grow and develop at different rates.

Height

The height you reach largely depends on your parents. If they are both tall, it is likely that you will be tall, too.

Developing skills

Crawling starts at about 10 months.

Walking begins at about 15 months.

Speaking with words in sentences begins at about two.

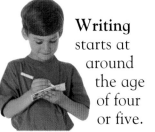

Writing starts at around the age of four or five.

Riding a bike is often mastered by the age of five or six.

Find out more   Animals 17   Early humans 49

Science and Technology

Human body: senses

Sight, sound, touch, smell, and taste – your five senses tell your brain what is happening around you and help to keep you safe.

The five senses

Touch
A rabbit is soft to the touch, but a hot pan can burn.

Sight
Your sight lets you thread a needle, and warns you not to touch a prickly cactus.

Sound
Sound lets us enjoy music. But it also warns us of danger, like a buzzing bee.

Sound

Touch

Sight

Smell

Taste

Working together
Your senses often work together. When you cross the road, you use your eyes to see and your ears to hear.

Taste
Taste tells you that ice cream is good to eat, but soap is not!

Smell
Your sense of smell allows you to enjoy a rose. But it warns you of sour milk or rotten eggs.

Sight problems
Guide dogs are trained to help blind or partially sighted people get around.

Braille is a form of writing, which blind people "read" by touch.

Hearing problems
Sign language helps people who can't talk or hear to communicate.

Hearing aids help people who can't hear well.

Did you know?
Our sight is so sharp we can see a candle flame 1.6 km (1 mile) away in the dark!

Human body: skeleton

Science and Technology

Your skeleton has 208 bones! It gives you your human shape and protects your vital organs. Without bones and muscles you couldn't move.

Skull protects your brain.

Shoulder blade

Spine

Rib cage protects your heart and lungs

Elbow joint

Your hand has 27 bones.

Hip joint

Thigh bones are the longest bones.

Knee cap

Shin bone

Ankle joint

Your foot has 26 bones.

Bones
Bones are made of a hard, strong material called calcium. We get calcium from milk.

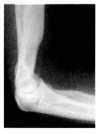
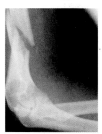

Broken bone
X-ray pictures

If a bone breaks, a doctor often wraps it in a plaster cast. This helps the bone grow together.

Long bones
Long bones are strong and light because they have air holes inside.

Inside a bone, magnified thousands of times

Bone joints
Ball and socket joint at shoulder

Hinge joint.
Joints are places where bones meet. They allow your body to bend.

False hip joint

False knee joint

False plastic joints are used to replace real joints that wear out.

Muscles
You have about 600 muscles. They work with your bones to help you move, skip, and jump.

Thigh muscles pull on the leg bones.

How muscles work
All muscles work in pairs.

1 The biceps muscle pulls the arm up.

2 The triceps muscle pulls the arm down.

Biceps muscle

Triceps muscle

Find out more Skeletons 128   Sport 135

Science and Technology

Human body: skin

Your hair keeps in heat and protects your scalp.

Your made-to-measure skin is waterproof, elastic, and tough. It protects your body, keeping your insides in and harmful germs out.

Skin uses

Skin
Skin is dead on the outside. Dry specks brush off our bodies every day. New skin grows underneath.

Old age
As you become older, your skin begins to sag and wrinkle.

Skin is waterproof. It protects you when you wash or go swimming.

If you are cold, the hairs on your skin stand up and trap air to keep you warm.

Skin is stretchy and moves when you do.

Hair
There are small hairs all over your body.

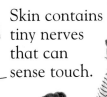

Eyebrows stop sweat dripping into your eyes.

Skin contains tiny nerves that can sense touch.

Did you know?
Your skin weighs about 3 kg (7 lbs). That's as much as a small bag of potatoes!

When you are hot, your skin sweats salt water to cool you down.

Sun block

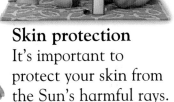

Skin senses heat, cold, moisture, and pain.

Skin protection
It's important to protect your skin from the Sun's harmful rays.

Hair
The hair on your head can come in any shape, length, and colour. Hair helps to keep you warm.

Fingerprint
The skin on everybody's fingertips has tiny ridges. These make unique patterns called fingerprints.

Find out more Insects of the world 87   Sport 135

83

Science and Technology

Human body: systems

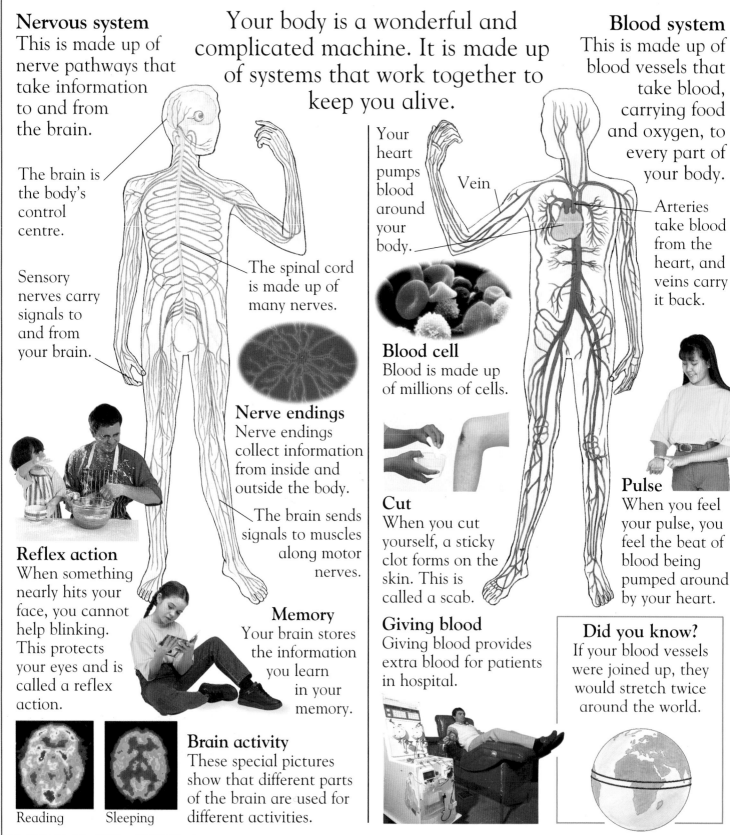

Your body is a wonderful and complicated machine. It is made up of systems that work together to keep you alive.

Nervous system
This is made up of nerve pathways that take information to and from the brain.

The brain is the body's control centre.

Sensory nerves carry signals to and from your brain.

The spinal cord is made up of many nerves.

Nerve endings
Nerve endings collect information from inside and outside the body.

The brain sends signals to muscles along motor nerves.

Reflex action
When something nearly hits your face, you cannot help blinking. This protects your eyes and is called a reflex action.

Memory
Your brain stores the information you learn in your memory.

Brain activity
These special pictures show that different parts of the brain are used for different activities.

Reading   Sleeping

Blood system
This is made up of blood vessels that take blood, carrying food and oxygen, to every part of your body.

Your heart pumps blood around your body.

Vein

Arteries take blood from the heart, and veins carry it back.

Blood cell
Blood is made up of millions of cells.

Cut
When you cut yourself, a sticky clot forms on the skin. This is called a scab.

Giving blood
Giving blood provides extra blood for patients in hospital.

Pulse
When you feel your pulse, you feel the beat of blood being pumped around by your heart.

Did you know?
If your blood vessels were joined up, they would stretch twice around the world.

Find out more — Food and eating 70 — Hospitals and doctors 79

Incas

Inca toy

This pottery dog belonged to an Inca child.

The Incas were people who lived in South America over 500 years ago. They ruled a great and wealthy empire.

Inca life

Gold was used to make precious goods, such as this gold llama.

Machu Picchu
The Incas were expert builders. This ancient city was built high up in the mountains of Peru.

Stone ruins of houses and temples

Flat terraces cut into the hillside.

Food grown on terraces.

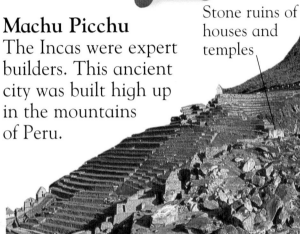

Music was very popular. These panpipes made a soft sound.

Religious ceremonies took place in special temples. Animals were often sacrificed.

Tools
Tools were made from wood, stone, bone, and wool.

Sling for hunting

Quinine for medicine

Plants
Plants were grown for food and medicines.

Hoe for farming

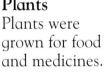
Maize

Potato

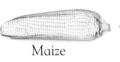
Snakeroot for stomach ache

Llama
Llamas were used to carry goods up and down mountains.

Gods and goddesses, like this statue of the goddess of farming, were important.

Did you know?
The Incas did not use writing. They recorded things on knotted strings called quipus.

Spanish conquest
In the 1530s, Spanish soldiers arrived in South America. They stole Inca gold, and sent it back to Spain.

Helmet

Spanish soldiers killed the Inca fighters quickly with their guns.

Gun

Dead bodies were carefully preserved. The Incas believed in life after death.

Find out more Ancient Egypt 13   Farming 64

Insects

Types of insect

Damselflies are expert fliers and dart through the air.

Beetles have hard wing cases to protect their delicate wings.

Flies have two wings that beat so fast, they buzz.

Butterflies and moths have four patterned wings.

They crawl, fly, buzz, and sting – insects may be small, but there are over a million kinds, more than any other animal in the world.

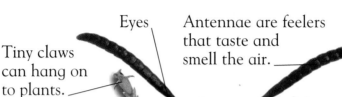

Eyes

Antennae are feelers that taste and smell the air.

Tiny claws can hang on to plants.

Wasp
All insects have three sections to their bodies and six legs – just like this wasp.

The head is the first part of the body.

The thorax is the middle part of the body.

The abdomen is the end part of the body.

The six legs bend at the joints.

Wings

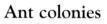
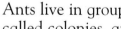

Ant colonies
Ants live in groups called colonies, and share out the work between them.

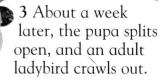

Growing up
Many insects change shape as they grow. This is called metamorphosis.

Ladybird egg

Larva

Pupa

Ladybird

1 A worm-like larva hatches from the egg. It feeds and grows.

2 The fully grown larva makes a hard case, called a pupa, around itself.

3 About a week later, the pupa splits open, and an adult ladybird crawls out.

Find out more Butterflies and moths 36 Insects of the world 87

Insects of the world

Insects live everywhere in the world except in the sea. They make their homes in trees, in the ground, in buildings, and even on us!

Did you know?
Whirlygig beetles have a set of upper eyes to see above the water, and a set of lower eyes to keep watch underwater!

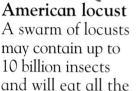

American locust
A swarm of locusts may contain up to 10 billion insects and will eat all the plants in its path.

Great diving beetle
This European pond dweller is fierce – it will even attack frogs.

Chequered skipper
This butterfly can survive in the freezing Arctic lands. It eats grass.

Robber fly
This fly lives near beehives in South America. It kills bees in mid-air and eats them.

ARCTIC OCEAN
EUROPE
NORTH AMERICA
ASIA
ATLANTIC OCEAN
AFRICA
PACIFIC OCEAN
SOUTH AMERICA
INDIAN OCEAN
AUSTRALASIA
ANTARCTICA

Asian violin beetle
This beetle is totally flat! It lives between thin layers of fungi on tree trunks.

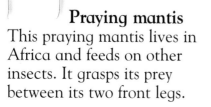

Head louse
This head louse, magnified many times, lives on human heads. It feeds on dead skin.

Praying mantis
This praying mantis lives in Africa and feeds on other insects. It grasps its prey between its two front legs.

Damselfly
This damselfly lives in southern Europe. It flies over water, feeding on flies.

Cockroach
Cockroaches live almost anywhere. They are scavengers and eat anything from paper to dead animals.

Goliath beetle
The Goliath is the heaviest beetle in the world. It lives in the African rainforest, eating tropical fruit.

Find out more   Human body: skin 83   Insects 86

Inventions

Electricity
Many new inventions followed the discovery of electricity in 1831.

Electric fires are quicker than making a coal fire.

Electric light is safer than candle light or gas lamps.

Electric irons were first used 100 years ago.

The wheel, X-rays, computer games – inventions may change our lives, or simply be fun. They are new ideas that do a job in a different way.

Transport
The need to travel has led to many great inventions.

Axle

Wooden crossbar

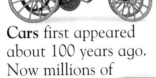

Cars first appeared about 100 years ago. Now millions of people drive.

Wheels are used on many kinds of vehicles. They were invented 5,000 years ago.

Planes were box-shaped at first. Today, they are fast, large, and sleek.

Medicine
Medical inventions help people to live longer, healthier, and more active lives.

False teeth help people who have lost their real teeth to eat.

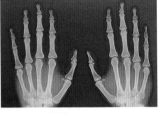

X-rays can help doctors to see inside our bodies without cutting them open.

Stethoscopes, invented in 1855, are used to listen to our heart or lungs.

Communications
Modern inventions have helped people to speak to each other over long distances.

Telephones are a way of sending sounds along wires.

Satellite dishes send and receive messages from all around the world.

Entertainment
Modern inventions have brought entertainment into the home.

Television is the most popular kind of home entertainment.

Computer games are small and light so that children can carry them around.

Compact discs play music that sounds as though it is playing live.

Did you know?
Thomas Edison, the inventor of the light bulb, was once expelled from school for laziness!

(1847–1931)

Find out more ▸ Computers 42   Machines 92

Life in the Past

Knights

Did you know?

A full suit of armour weighed about the same as a six-year-old child.

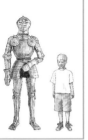

Knights were medieval soldiers in armour who fought on horseback for a lord or a king. They lived from about 1,000 years ago.

Types of armour

An **Italian knight** in 1380 had armour that covered only part of his body.

Weapons and armour

In battle, knights used dangerous weapons made of iron and steel. A suit of armour protected them from cuts and blows.

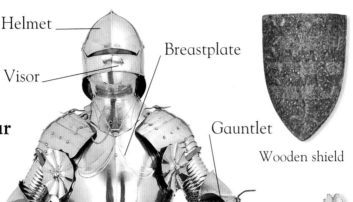

Helmet

Visor

Breastplate

Gauntlet

Wooden shield

Sword

Close-fitting chain mail

Sword belt

Spur

Leg armour

Short axe

Copper and steel sword

An **English knight** in 1590 was totally protected by his armour.

Horse armour

Some knights used armour for their horses, too.

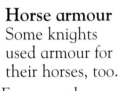

Face guard

Neck guard

Spike

Eye guard

Nose guard

Spurs

Samurai warriors were Japanese knights. Their metal armour was laced together with silk.

Tournaments

In times of peace, knights took part in jousting tournaments. They charged at each other on horseback, carrying lances.

Lance

Shield

Horses draped with knights' colours.

Helmets

Tournaments were very colourful. Many knights wore unusual helmets.

Italian helmet

Helmet with eagle's beak

Find out more Castles 38 Festivals 65

Science and Technology

Light

Light rays

Light rays can travel through some materials.

Transparent

materials like glass allow light rays to travel through them.

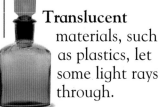

Translucent

materials, such as plastics, let some light rays through.

Opaque materials, like wrapping paper, do not let any light rays through.

Reflection

When light rays bounce off shiny things, like still water, they make a reflection.

It's impossible to think of a world without light. Light is a kind of energy that you can see. Without it, nothing can live or grow.

Light and shadow

Light travels in straight lines called rays. When light rays hit something solid, the light is blocked and a shadow forms on the other side.

The Sun is our planet's most important source of light.

Long shadow

Hand shadows

It's fun to make shadows with our hands.

Types of light

Electric light

is powered by electricity and used in buildings and outdoors.

Candlelight

was used to light homes in the past.

Glow-worms

make light from chemicals in their body.

Lightning is a kind of electricity. It makes a flash of bright light.

Did you know?

People still tell the time by using the shadows on sundials.

Plants and light

Plants need light to make food for themselves. They die if they are left in the dark.

Plants grow towards light.

Leaf in light   Leaf in dark

Fireworks explode to make a beautiful, chemical light.

Find out more
 Colour 40
Sun and stars 137

World of Nature

Living things

Stones do not need air to breathe. They are not living.

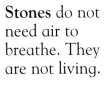

Animals and plants are both living things. But there is one big difference – plants can make food for themselves, while animals have to find it.

Sunflower makes seeds.

Animals
All animals move around to find food for themselves, just like this chicken.

Chicken breathes oxygen.

Plants
Like all plants, sunflowers are alive. They stay in one place and make food for themselves.

Chickens peck the ground for food.

Chickens have young called chicks.

Plants use water, air, and sunlight to make their own food.

Sunflower is rooted in the ground.

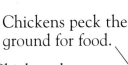

Dog

Spider

Sea urchin

Sponge

Bird

Maize

Cactus

Thistle

Seaweed

Moss

Did you know?
Coral may look like a lump of rock, but it is made of millions of tiny animals.

Ingredients for life

Water is an important part of every plant and animal.

Air helps plants and animals to make energy for themselves.

Light helps plants to grow. Without plants, animals would die from hunger.

Find out more Amphibians 11   Trees 143

Machines

Did you know?
The Greek scientist Archimedes, invented a pulley that would allow one man to pull a ship in or out of water.

People have always used machines to make their lives easier. Simple machines like wheels, pulleys, and levers help us in dozens of ways every day.

Lever
Levers help lift loads. They have a rod or bar that turns around a pivot.

This corkscrew uses levers to lift a cork out of a bottle.

Pivot

Rod

Scissors are two levers joined together.

Pivot

Rod

Scales
This pair of scales is a lever.

Pivot

Rod

Bicycle
Bicycles are machines that use pedal power to carry us faster and further than walking.

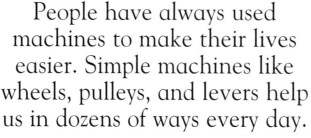

The wheel spins round on the axle.

Gear
Gears are wheels with teeth that fit into each other. Gear wheels change the speed at which parts of a machine work.

Hand whisk

The gears in a watch make the different hands move at different speeds.

Inside a watch

Gears give power on hills.

Pedals are levers to push against.

Wheel
Wheels turn round an axle. They are used to move things smoothly.

Slope
We use slopes in many machines. Rolling something up a slope is often easier than lifting it straight up in the air.

Pulley
A pulley uses a wheel and a rope to lift very heavy loads.

Pulley

Cranes use pulleys to raise and lower loads.

Find out more Bicycles 29   Science 122

Magnets

Magnet uses

Fridge magnets are used to hold notes on a fridge.

Metal detectors use magnets to find metal objects under the ground.

Magnets are used in spacecraft to stop things floating around.

Phones, and many other electrical machines, use magnets.

Magnets are made from iron or steel. They look like ordinary metal, but they have the power to pull things towards them or push them away.

Magnetic poles
The two ends of a magnet are called the north and south poles.

Around each pole is a magnetic field.

North pole

North pole

South pole

South pole

South pole

North pole

North pole

South pole

Magnetic forces pull two different poles together.

Did you know?
Electromagnets are very powerful. They can even lift up old cars!

The magnetic field is a powerful, invisible magnetic force.

Magnetic forces push the same poles apart.

Magnetic materials
Magnets only attract certain kinds of metals, such as iron and steel.

Steel spoon

Man-made magnet

Natural magnet
Lodestone is a natural magnetic rock. Most magnets are man-made.

Lodestone

Iron nails

Steel paper-clips

Magnetic Earth
The biggest magnet of all is the Earth. It has two magnetic poles that create a magnetic force around Earth.

Magnetic north pole

Magnetic south pole

Compass
Compass needles always point to the magnetic north pole.

Compass

A ship's compass helps sailors to find their way.

Northern lights
This light show in the sky is created by the magnetic force around the Earth.

Find out more ➤ North America 102   Pirates 108

Mammals

Many of the animals we know best are mammals. Cats, cows, monkeys, and mice are all mammals. So are human beings.

Large eyes see well, even in the dark.

Long whiskers touch and feel.

Sharp teeth catch and chew food.

Leopard
The different parts of a leopard's body help it survive. Other land mammals have similar kinds of bodies.

Did you know?
The biggest mammal in the world is the blue whale. It is as heavy as 2,000 people!

Marsupial mammals
Some mammals, like this kangaroo, have a furry pouch on their stomach. Their babies spend many months growing in here.

Long tail for balance

Strong claws help to climb trees.

Dappled fur for camouflage among the trees

Mammal facts

Echidna

Mammals have fur, hair, or even spines on their bodies.

Wolf

Mammals are warm to the touch. They need food for energy.

Chimp

Mammals have larger brains than other animals.

Mammal babies feed on their mothers' milk.

Giraffes

Mother and baby
Baby mammals grow inside their mother's body until they are born.

Newborn puppy

Baby puppies grow bigger on their mothers' milk.

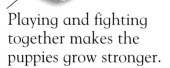
Playing and fighting together makes the puppies grow stronger.

Find out more ▷ 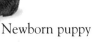 Animals 17   Mammals of the world 95

Mammals of the world

There are only about 4,000 different kinds of mammal, but they live in every part of the world – on land, in the sea, and in the air.

Reindeer
Reindeer live in the snowy northern wastelands. Some are kept for meat and leather.

Otter
Otters are expert divers and live and feed in the rivers of North America.

Porcupine
Porcupines live in Europe, Africa, and America. They raise their sharp quills to protect themselves.

Bat
Bats are the only mammals that can fly. They live in large groups in caves all over the world.

Bush-baby
Bush-babies have huge eyes. They hunt at night among the trees of the African rainforests.

Dolphin
Dolphins are found in all the oceans of the world. They live in large groups called herds.

ARCTIC OCEAN

EUROPE

NORTH AMERICA

ASIA

PACIFIC OCEAN

AFRICA

ATLANTIC OCEAN

INDIAN OCEAN

SOUTH AMERICA

AUSTRALASIA

ANTARCTICA

Brown bear
The European bear climbs trees to raid bees' nests for their honey.

Mountain goat
These goats are very surefooted. They live on mountain slopes in North America.

Zebra
Zebras live on the grassy plains of Africa. Their stripes help to camouflage them.

Mouse
Mice are found all over the world. They often live in people's homes, eating crumbs.

Rhinoceros
Rhinos are found in Africa and Asia. They use their fierce-looking horns to defend themselves.

Did you know?
When they are attacked, skunks spray a horrible-smelling liquid at their enemy, and then run away.

Find out more Animal families 15 Mammals 94

Maps

World map

1 A globe is the most accurate map of the world.

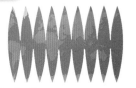

2 A flat map is made by flattening out the globe.

3 The gaps are filled in with extra bits of land and sea.

Maps are pictures that show places, such as towns, from above. We use maps to find our way around.

Abruzzo National Park, southern Italy

A **compass** always points to the north. It helps you find your way with a map.

Map reading
You must be able to read a map to find your way.

Symbols
The special signs on a map are symbols. A symbol represents something real. Symbols are explained in a key.

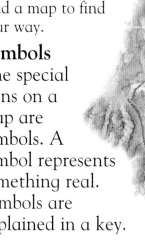

Beech and pine forest

Lake Barrea

Pecasseroli

Mount Marsicano

River Sangro

Opi

Lake Barrea

River Mella

N

This symbol shows you where north is on the map.

Did you know?
Space satellites take photos of the Earth to help people make more accurate maps.

Key

 A very beautiful place

 A good viewpoint

 Tourist information

 Mount Marsicano

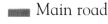 Main road

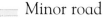 Minor road

Footpath

Types of map

Street maps name all the streets in a town or city.

Weather maps show the weather in different places.

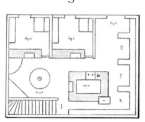

Underground maps show where the train lines go.

Floor plans show you the layout of a building.

Road maps help drivers plan a journey.

Find out more 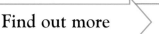 Explorers 61 Magnets 93

Science and Technology

Materials

Steel is strong, glass is clear, cotton is soft – every material has special qualities. Everything we use is made from materials just right for the job.

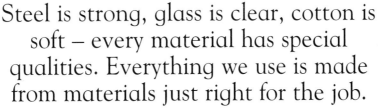

Cotton plant

Cotton is turned into thread to make clothes.

Did you know?
Nowadays, jumpers can be knitted from recycled plastic!

Cotton
Some materials, such as cotton, are found naturally. Others are made in factories.

Glass
Glass is useful because you can see through it. It is made from sand, limestone, and soda.

Steel
Steel is a hard, strong metal. It consists of iron, carbon, and limestone melted down together.

Plastic
Plastic is strong and does not rot or rust. It is made from heated oil.

Materials for different jobs

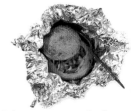

Aluminium foil can withstand high temperatures. It is used for cooking.

Natural sponges soak up lots of water. They are good for washing with.

Polyester fabric is made in factories. It is soft and often used to make teddy bears.

Wood is naturally hard and strong. It is often used to make furniture.

New materials
New artificial materials are being invented all the time.

Lycra clothes fit comfortably.

Bullet-proof vest made of Kevlar

Recycling
Some materials, like glass, can be recycled to make new products.

Recycled glass

Moon

Moon machines

This **moon buggy** is used by astronauts to move around the moon quickly.

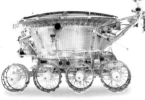

This **lunokhod** is a Russian vehicle. It was put on the moon to take photographs.

A **lunar module** carried astronauts from their spacecraft to the moon's surface.

Did you know?
It's possible to jump six times higher on the moon than on Earth due to the weaker gravity there!

The moon is a ball of rock that circles the Earth. It is our nearest neighbour in space. Astronauts have landed on the moon and mapped its surface.

Moon surface
There are flat plains, valleys, mountains, and craters on the moon's surface.

Low land filled in by the lava of ancient volcanoes.

Moon from Earth
The moon looks bright because one side is lit by the Sun.

Astronaut

Dusty surface

Bare rocks

Climate
Because there is no wind or rain on the moon, flags won't fly and footprints will never disappear.

Astronaut's footprint

American flag is held up by wire.

Craters
Craters are big holes on the moon's surface.

Moon phases
As the moon travels around the Earth, we see different parts of its sunlit side. This gives us the phases of the moon.

Full moon

Crescent moon

Half moon

Find out more Planets 109   Space travel 133

World of Nature

Mountains

The high, rocky slopes of mountains are battered by cold winds and covered by heavy snow. They make a harsh habitat for animals and plants.

Mountain plants
To survive the harsh conditions, mountain plants have special shapes and parts.

Trees cannot grow above the tree line.

Lichen
Lichens grow high up, because they can survive extreme cold.

Coniferous forests grow on the higher slopes.

Poor, thin soil

Mountain animals

Vultures' large wings allow them to glide on the strong mountain winds.

A **bobcat's** spotted coat helps it to blend in with its rocky mountain home.

Chinchillas have thick fur coats to protect them from the cold.

Deciduous forests grow on the lower slopes.

Rhododendron
Thick, shiny leaves save this plant from the cold.

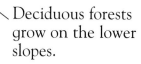

Bell heather
The tiny leaves of this heather can withstand strong winds.

Rock-rose
Rock-roses grow close to the ground to stay out of the wind.

Mountain goats have specially shaped hooves to help them clamber over rocks.

Did you know?
In 1963, a volcanic island suddenly appeared in the sea. Called Surtsey, it is now home to plants.

Volcano
When volcanoes erupt, they shoot out molten rock. This can build a mountain in less than a week!

Find out more Asia 20   Plants 110

Life Today

Music

Music is a pattern of sounds made by musical instruments, and human voices. People enjoy different kinds of music all over the world.

Types of music

Popular music is fun and catchy. It is good for dancing to.

Nursery rhymes are simple songs for young children.

Choral music is usually religious. It is sung by groups called choirs.

Classical music is written by composers for instruments in an orchestra.

Music in the home

Most people listen to recorded music at home.

Compact disc   Personal stereo

Radio

African music

Music is played differently around the world. African music has strong rhythms – perfect for dancing.

Wooden drums beat out the rhythm.

Musical notes

Music is written on a set of lines, using notes instead of words.

Dancing to the beat

Moroccan music

Moroccan music is often based around folk stories and dance.

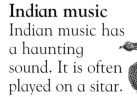

Indian music

Indian music has a haunting sound. It is often played on a sitar.

Mexican music

Mexican bands play traditional folk music on violins and guitars.

Did you know?

The German composer Beethoven was only three when he performed his first piece of music!

Find out more ▶   Festivals 65   Musical instruments 101

Life Today

Musical instruments

Did you know?
In 1454, a French orchestra hid in a giant pie to surprise guests at a party!

Most instruments belong to one of five family groups. Each group makes its musical sound in a different way.

Percussion
These instruments make a sound when they are hit or shaken.

Maracas are rattles. They make a swishing sound.

Strings
Stringed instruments can be bowed, plucked, or strummed.

A **double bass** is one of the largest instruments. It has a very deep sound.

Sitars are Indian stringed instruments.

Bow scrapes strings

Four strings

Tambourines have jingling metal discs.

Triangles make a clear, tinkling sound.

Electronic instruments
These use electricity to make sounds.

Electric pianos can make the sound of many different instruments.

Chamber group
Stringed instruments are often played in small musical groups.

Wooden body

Metal spike to rest on

Electric drums can only be heard through loudspeakers.

Woodwind
Woodwind instruments make a sound when you blow air inside them.

Recorders are one of the simplest woodwind instruments.

Flutes are made of metal.

Oboes have keys for fingers. The mouthpiece is made from a reed.

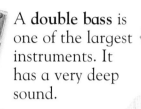

Accordions work by air being blown in with bellows.

Brass
Musicians blow and vibrate their lips to make these brass instruments sound.

French horns have long pipes that end with a large bell.

Digeridoos are made from a hollow branch.

Trumpets have a narrow tube bent round twice.

Find out more Sound 129 Theatre 139

Continents of the World

North America

Canada and Alaska

North America reaches as far north as the Arctic Ocean. Its rivers, peaks, forests, and lakes are a haven for wildlife.

Did you know?
- Canada is the second biggest country in the world.
- Greenland is the world's largest island.

Tundra
In the far north is a frozen, treeless plain called the tundra.

Queen Elizabeth Islands

Baffin Island

GREENLAND (DENMARK)

Greenland
Greenland lies in the Arctic Ocean. Much of the land is covered in ice.

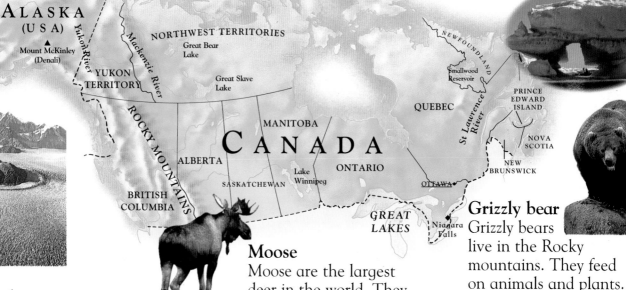

ALASKA (USA)

Mount McKinley (Denali)

Yukon River

YUKON TERRITORY

Mackenzie River

NORTHWEST TERRITORIES

Great Bear Lake

Great Slave Lake

NEWFOUNDLAND

Smallwood Reservoir

QUEBEC

St Laurence River

PRINCE EDWARD ISLAND

NOVA SCOTIA

NEW BRUNSWICK

ROCKY MOUNTAINS

ALBERTA

BRITISH COLUMBIA

SASKATCHEWAN

MANITOBA

CANADA

Lake Winnipeg

ONTARIO

OTTAWA

GREAT LAKES

Niagara Falls

Glacier
Alaska has huge rivers of ice called glaciers.

Moose
Moose are the largest deer in the world. They feed only on plants.

Grizzly bear
Grizzly bears live in the Rocky mountains. They feed on animals and plants.

Northern lights
These glowing lights can be seen in the skies above Canada.

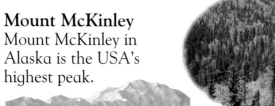

Mount McKinley
Mount McKinley in Alaska is the USA's highest peak.

Pine forests
Forests cover more than one-third of Canada. Many animals shelter here.

Niagara Falls
The Niagara Falls in Canada are made up of two thundering waterfalls.

Find out more ▷ Forests 73   Magnets 93

Continents of the World

North America: culture

Canada and Alaska
This huge land has a small population. Most of the people live in cities in the warmer south.

Fishing
Fishing in Canada's lakes and seas is a popular sport and an important industry.

Culture
The **maple leaf** is the national emblem of Canada.

Forestry, Canada
Forestry is one of Canada's most important industries. The pine trees are made into timber and paper.

Truck carries logs to sawmill

Felled trees

Ice hockey is a popular winter sport, and is followed by many Canadians.

Native Americans were the first people to live in Canada.

French-speaking Canadians live in the east, in the province of Quebec.

Rodeos celebrate the skills of cowboys who ride wild horses.

Farming
Canada's farmers raise cattle or grow huge fields of wheat on the prairies.

Industry
Mining is important. Most of the world's zinc and nickel is mined here.

Zinc   Nickel

Oil is drilled in Alaska. It is then transported south along the world's longest pipeline.

Find out more Farming 64   Rocks and minerals 120

North America

USA and Mexico

With mountains in the north and deserts in the south, North America has some of the most spectacular scenery in the world.

Rocky Mountains
The Rockies stretch for 4,800 km (3,000 miles) down the western side of the USA.

Monument Valley
These sandstone rocks have been carved by winds in the Painted Desert, Utah.

Great Lakes
The five Great Lakes make up the largest area of fresh water in the world.

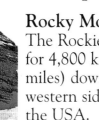

States
1 VERMONT
2 NEW JERSEY
3 DELAWARE
4 MARYLAND
5 CONNECTICUT
6 NEW HAMPSHIRE
7 MASSACHUSETTS
8 RHODE ISLAND

N

WASHINGTON
OREGON
IDAHO
MONTANA
NORTH DAKOTA
SOUTH DAKOTA
WYOMING
NEBRASKA
MINNESOTA
WISCONSIN
MICHIGAN
Lake Superior
Lake Huron
Lake Ontario
Lake Michigan
Lake Erie
NEW YORK
MAINE
ROCKY MOUNTAINS
CALIFORNIA
NEVADA
UTAH
COLORADO
KANSAS
IOWA
ILLINOIS
INDIANA
OHIO
PENNSYLVANIA
WEST VIRGINIA
WASHINGTON D.C.
U S A
Death Valley
Grand Canyon
ARIZONA
NEW MEXICO
OKLAHOMA
MISSOURI
ARKANSAS
KENTUCKY
TENNESSEE
VIRGINIA
NORTH CAROLINA
SOUTH CAROLINA
SONORAN DESERT
TEXAS
LOUISIANA
MISSISSIPPI
ALABAMA
GEORGIA
Okefenokee Swamp
FLORIDA
EVERGLADES
HAWAII
M E X I C O
MEXICO CITY

Everglades
This vast tropical marsh in Florida is home to animals such as alligators.

Collared lizard
This lizard manages to survive in the dry deserts.

Grand Canyon
This deep, rocky gorge has been cut out in Arizona by the River Colorado.

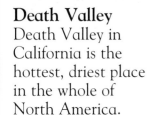

Death Valley
Death Valley in California is the hottest, driest place in the whole of North America.

Sonoran Desert
This desert lies between the USA and Mexico. It is famous for its giant cacti.

Okefenokee swamp
This freshwater swamp in southern Georgia is a safe refuge for wildlife.

Continents of the World

North America: culture

USA and Mexico
The USA and Mexico are large, modern countries, but they both have strong traditions and cultures.

New York
This is the largest city in the USA and is the country's business centre.

Silicon valley

Silicon chip

Chrysler building

Industry
The USA's famous computer industry is in Silicon Valley, California.

Farming
The prairies in central America are very fertile. They are used to grow wheat and other cereals.

Culture

Baseball is the national sport of the USA.

Hollywood, in Los Angeles, is the film capital of the world.

Rock and roll was invented in the USA.

Jazz music began in the southern states of America.

Ancient ruins

Ancient temples were built in Mexico many hundreds of years ago.

Traditional crafts
Many traditional goods are still made throughout the USA and Mexico.

Mexican masks

American quilt

Navajo rug

Tourism
Millions of people visit North America every year to see its famous landmarks and scenery.

Florida

White House

Las Vegas

Find out more Grasslands 77 Incas 85

Science and Technology

Oil

Oil is formed over millions of years. It is found deep inside the Earth, and is pumped out to make many different kinds of fuel.

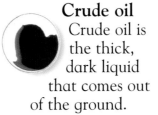

Fuels from oil
Different parts of the crude oil are used to make other fuels.

Propane gas is stored in bottles and tanks and used for cooking and heating.

Paraffin oil is used in lamps and heaters. It is also mixed into paint to make it smooth.

Oil is used as a lubricant. It helps machine parts to slide against each other.

Petrol is one of the most important products of oil. It is a fuel for cars.

Oil rig
Drills on an oil rig dig deep into the sea bed. The oil and gas are then pumped up and taken to the shore by pipes.

Crude oil
Crude oil is the thick, dark liquid that comes out of the ground.

Nodding donkey
This is a small oil rig that pumps up oil found under land.

Gases are burnt off.

Crane lifts heavy drill parts.

Workers live on an oil rig for weeks at a time.

The oil rig's concrete legs rest on the sea bed.

Drilling
Holes, called wells, are drilled deep underground to collect the oil.

Drill bit
The bits have strong steel teeth to cut into hard ground.

Oil refinery
Crude oil is taken to a refinery. Here, it is heated until it separates into different parts.

Heating towers

Waste gases are burnt off.

Did you know?
Drill bits get so worn down by the hard rock they drill into, that they need replacing twice a day.

Find out more   Conservation 43   Materials 97

Painting

Types of painting

A **self-portrait** is an artist's painting of him- or herself.

Murals are large paintings that are painted on a wall.

Portraits are pictures of people. They are not always true to life!

Abstract paintings use lines, shapes, and colours.

Landscapes are paintings of outdoor scenes.

People have painted pictures for thousands of years, creating works of art on walls, wood, paper, or canvas.

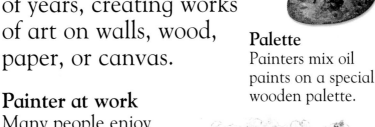

Palette
Painters mix oil paints on a special wooden palette.

Painter at work
Many people enjoy painting as a hobby. They often work outside, painting from nature.

Easel for supporting the picture.

Paintbox

Painting surfaces
Artists paint on different surfaces, such as paper or canvas.

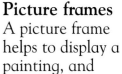

Paper   Canvas

Picture frames
A picture frame helps to display a painting, and protects it as it hangs on a wall.

Paints and inks
Artists create pictures with various materials. This makes their paintings look very different.

Pen-and-ink drawing

Oil painting

Watercolour painting

Find out more   Australasia: culture 28   Colour 40

Life in the Past

Pirates

Pirates were the robbers of the seas. They attacked ships and stole their cargo, and sometimes even the ship itself!

Pirate ships
Pirate ships were small and fast. They were only recognizable by their unusual flag!

Navigation
Pirates used the Sun, stars, instruments, and maps to find their way at sea.

Figurehead
Sailors believed that a figurehead on the boat would protect them.

The Jolly Roger – the pirates' flag

Death's skull

Crossed swords

Map

Telescope

Compass

Pirate attack
Pirates attacked ships and then pulled them close with iron hooks.

Cannon

Iron hook

Pirate's life
Many pirates led awful lives. At sea, they ate hard biscuits and limes to stay healthy.

Limes   Biscuits

Punishment
If pirates were caught, they were hanged. Their bodies were hung in an iron cage to warn others.

Iron cage

Treasure
Pirates attacked merchant ships to steal their valuable cargo. They shared out the lost treasure between them.

Treasure chest

Did you know?
When the pirate Blackbeard went into battle, he set fire to string in his hair!

Ankle chains

Handcuffs

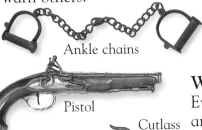

Pistol

Cutlass

Weapons
Every pirate was armed with a pistol and a short, sharp sword called a cutlass.

Silver coins   Rings

Diamond and amethyst necklace

Find out more Maps 96   Ships and boats 127

Planets

Planets are huge balls of rock, metal, and gas that travel around a star in space. The Earth is one of a family of nine planets that circle the Sun.

Did you know?
Saturn has 18 moons in its rings – more than any other planet!

Jupiter
Jupiter is the biggest planet. It is made up of hot, runny rock and swirling gases.

Cold surface

Mercury
Mercury is closest to the Sun. It's boiling hot by day and freezing cold at night.

Jupiter is larger than all the other planets put together.

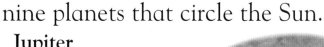

A red spot is a great storm.

Saturn
Saturn's shining rings are made up of ice, rocks, and dust.

Venus
Venus is the hottest planet. It is covered in thick clouds of gas.

Asteroids and meteorites
These are tiny planets made up of rocks and metal.

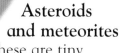

Earth
Earth is the only planet with air and water, vital to all living things.

Mars
Mars is very cold, and covered in dead volcanoes, craters, and dusty red soil.

Asteroids are larger than meteorites.

Pluto
Pluto is the smallest planet. It lies furthest from the Sun.

Neptune
Neptune has cold winds that blow as fast as Concorde.

Uranus
Uranus is covered with a thick layer of beautiful blue-green gas.

Meteorite fragments

Solar System
Four planets lie close to the Sun. Five planets lie much further away.

Sun Venus
Earth
Mercury Mars Jupiter Saturn Uranus Neptune Pluto

Find out more ➤ Moon 98 Sun and stars 137

World of Nature

Plants

There are over 425,000 different plants in the world, and they come in every shape and size – from delicate seaweeds to towering trees.

Types of plant

Cacti grow in hot, dry areas and store water in their stems.

Mosses grow in moist soils. They never flower.

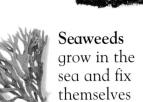

Seaweeds grow in the sea and fix themselves to rocks.

Grasses are an important food for many animals.

Trees are the biggest plants. Their trunks are really very large stems.

Flowers make seeds.

Shrub
All plants have the same basic parts, just like this *Skimmia japonica* shrub.

Leaves make food for the whole plant.

Food
Plants use air, water, the green in their leaves called chlorophyll, and the Sun's energy to make food.

Stems carry water and food to the whole plant.

Roots take up water from the soil and hold the plant in the ground.

First leaves open.

Seed leaves wither.

Sprouting seed

Beechnut seeds

1 The seed soaks up water, swells, and splits.

2 A tiny root grows down into the soil.

Seed case

3 A shoot grows up towards the light.

Did you know?
Giant kelp seaweed grows so tall, it would reach higher than the Leaning Tower of Pisa in Italy!

Plants as food

Sweetcorn is made up of seeds.

Tarragon is a leaf. **A carrot** is a root.

Cabbage is a group of leaves.

Broccoli is a mix of flowers and stems!

Ginger is a root.

A tomato is a fruit.

Find out more ▶ Flowers 69   Fruits and seeds 75

World of Nature

Polar animals

Did you know?

The coats of Arctic foxes turn white in the winter to hide the animals in the snow.

Around the north and south poles it is bitterly cold and windy. But many animals have found different ways to survive here.

Migration

Reindeer migrate south from the Arctic in winter to find food and shelter.

Seal

Weddel seals spend winter under the Antarctic ice sheet. They breathe through holes in the ice.

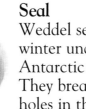

Penguin

Emperor penguins live on the Antarctic ice, huddling together in groups to keep warm. They can't fly, but are expert swimmers.

Flippers push the penguin through water.

Beak has feathers for warmth.

Snowy owls also travel south in winter. They feed on Arctic rabbits.

Wolf

Wolves have hairs under their paws to give them a good grip on the ice.

Closely packed feathers

Musk oxen move south from the Arctic in the winter to find grazing.

Polar bear

Polar bears have thick, oily coats to keep out the cold. They are the only mammals to live on the Arctic ice.

Feet are small to cut down heat loss.

Krill

Krill are tiny shrimp-like animals that live in the seas around Antarctica.

Walrus

A thick layer of fatty blubber keeps the walrus warm in the cold Arctic seas.

Moose travel north to the Arctic shore in the summer to escape all the flies in the south.

Polar lands

The polar lands lie around the north and south poles. The frozen ground and icy climate make them a hard place for plants to grow.

Antarctica
No-one lives in the Antarctic, but scientists visit to study the land and its wildlife.

Polar plants

Mosses grow in thick cushions. This protects them from icy winds.

Icefield
A lot of the land in the polar regions is covered in huge areas of ice, called icefields.

Glaciers flow from the icefields.

Glaciers are rivers of ice that move slowly down mountain slopes.

The **Arctic wormwood** stores food in its roots to help it survive.

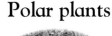

Grasses grow quickly in the spring when there are long periods of daylight.

Tundra
The tundra is the frozen land in the far north. The ice melts here in the summer, and a few plants manage to grow.

Life in the Arctic
People have lived in the Arctic for thousands of years. They have had to adapt their lifestyle to the harsh climate.

Primroses have long roots to help them survive.

Did you know?
The tallest ever iceberg was higher than St Paul's Cathedral, London.

Winter coat

Dog-pulled sleds make it possible to move goods across the ice.

Warm clothes are made from animal skins.

Husky dog

Sled

Fleabane grows only for a few weeks in the Arctic summer.

Find out more ➤   Antarctica 19   Polar animals 111

World of Nature

Rainforest animals

Flying animals

Morpho butterflies have bright colours to help them attract a mate.

Scarlet macaws have hooked beaks that can crack open nuts.

Toucans use their long beaks to pick fruit and steal other birds' eggs.

Fruit bats rest during the day in the forest canopy.

Monkeys howl, parrots shriek, and insects chirp – tropical rainforests are noisy places, and home to a huge variety of wildlife.

Spider monkey
Monkeys swing through the canopy, gripping the branches with their strong feet, hands, and tails.

Thick, woolly coat

Tree snake
These snakes live in trees near water. They eat frogs and lizards.

The monkey's tail can support it from a branch.

Baby monkey clings on to its mother.

Monkeys feed on tasty fruit and leaves.

Jaguar
The jaguar's coat helps to hide it in the dappled forest light.

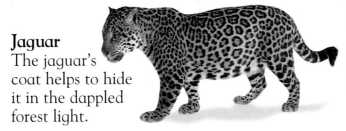

Did you know?
Scarlet macaws can tell each other apart by special patterns on each other's feathers.

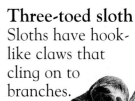

Tree frogs
Tree frogs spend their lives high up in the branches.

Three-toed sloth
Sloths have hook-like claws that cling on to branches.

Gecko
The gecko's clever camouflage hides it from hungry snakes.

Ants
These ants eat a fungus which grows on the leaves they cut and store.

Find out more Rainforests 114 South America 131

113

World of Nature

Rainforests

Forest flowers

Slipper orchids are pollinated by only one type of bee.

Shaving brush trees have strongly scented flowers to attract bats.

Steriphomas flowers are tube-shaped. Only long-tongued insects can feed on them.

The **hotlips plant** has beautiful bright red flowers.

Passifloras are creepers that grow quickly towards the light in the canopy above.

Tropical rainforests are hot, sticky places packed with trees and climbers. All the plants and daily rainfall make them dark and steamy.

Trees grow tall to reach the sun.

The forest roof, about 40 m (130 ft) above the ground, is called the canopy.

Thick leaves and branches

Leaves stay on the trees all year round.

Creepers climb up trees.

Young sapling

Did you know?
There are many plants and animals in the rainforests that have not yet been discovered by people.

Rainforest layers
A rainforest is like a tall building with many levels, as different plants grow to different heights.

Smaller trees grow lower down where it is shady.

Forest floor is dark and wet.

Rainforest tribes
The Txucuhamai tribe has lived in South American rainforests for thousands of years.

Forest fruit
Rainforest plants provide us with all sorts of delicious food to eat.

Bread fruit

Nutmeg

Cocoa

Ginger

Pineapple

Find out more Animals in danger 18 　　 Conservation 43

Life Today

Religion

There are five main world religions. Christians, Jews, and Muslims believe in one God, Hindus believe in many, and Buddhists do not worship a god.

The Bible is the Christian holy book.

Christianity

Christians worship one God. They believe that God's son, Jesus Christ, lived on Earth about 2,000 years ago.

Angels

Mary, mother of Jesus

The Christian symbol is a cross.

Judaism

Judaism was the first religion to believe in one God, about 4,000 years ago. Its followers are called Jews.

Men wear skullcaps.

Candles for a Jewish festival

The Torah is the holy book.

A shrine, for prayers at home

Hinduism

Hinduism is an Asian religion. The followers, called Hindus, worship many gods.

Snake mask to chase off evil

The Hindu God Shiva

Did you know?

Followers of Jainism believe in protecting all living things. They wear masks to stop insects going into their mouths.

Sacred words on an Islamic tile

The Koran is the Muslims' holy book.

Islam

The religion of Islam was started by a prophet, Muhammed. Its followers are called Muslims. They worship one God.

Muslims pray on a prayer mat.

Buddhism

Buddhism began in India. Its followers, called Buddhists, believe that they will be born again after they die.

The Buddhist wheel of life

Prayer wheel

The Buddha was a prince who became a monk.

Places of worship

Each religion has special buildings, where people get together to pray. They are guided by a religious leader.

Christian church

Muslim mosque

Buddhist temple

Hindu temple

Jewish synagogue

Reptiles

Lizards, tortoises, crocodiles, and snakes are all reptiles. Most of them live in warm places, have dry, scaly skin, and lay eggs on dry land.

Reptile families

Sinaloan milk snake

Snakes are expert hunters. They poison their prey or squeeze it to death.

Alligator snapping turtle

Turtles are excellent swimmers. They only come on land to lay their eggs.

Basilisk lizard

Lizards make up over half of all reptiles. They are small, quick, and feed on insects.

Hermann's tortoise

Tortoises live on land. Their hard shells protect them from their enemies.

The scales are like armour for protection.

Strong tail for swimming

Did you know?
Many snakes eat their food while it is still alive!

Crocodile
Crocodiles live and catch their food in rivers. Their bodies are perfect for hunting in water.

Baby caiman

Reptile eggs
Baby snakes cut their way out of their shell with a special tiny egg tooth.

Rat snake

Eye

Long, snapping jaws and sharp teeth catch prey.

Webbed feet move like paddles.

Baby reptiles
Unlike most reptiles, crocodiles take care of their babies for a few weeks after hatching.

Lizard tails
If a lizard's tail is grabbed by an enemy, it can break off, letting the lizard escape. A new tail soon grows back.

Tree skink

Broken tail

Newly grown tail

Garden lizard

Cold-blooded
Reptiles are cold-blooded. They need heat from the Sun to warm up and shady places to cool down.

Find out more ▸ Animals 17   Reptiles of the world 117

World of Nature

Reptiles of the world

Alligator
Alligators live in the swamps of North America. When resting, they open their mouths to cool down.

There are over 6,000 different kinds of reptile, and most of them live where it is warm. Some live in water, but many more prefer to stay on dry land.

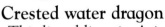

European grass snake
To escape its enemies, this snake lies upside down and pretends to be dead.

Soft-shelled turtle
This turtle lives in North America. It is usually found buried in mud in rivers and ponds.

Cobra
This cobra has a poisonous bite that can kill in minutes. It lives in Asia.

ARCTIC OCEAN
EUROPE
NORTH AMERICA
ASIA
ATLANTIC OCEAN
AFRICA
PACIFIC OCEAN
SOUTH AMERICA
INDIAN OCEAN
AUSTRALASIA
ANTARCTICA

Tegu lizard
This South American lizard has a tough skin made from horny scales.

Crested water dragon
This lizard lives in Asia and can run faster on two legs than it can on four.

Pricklenape agama
The agama lives in north African deserts. When food is scarce, it survives on fat in its tail.

Did you know?
When it's attacked, a horned toad squirts blood from its eyes to shock its enemies.

Chameleon
Chameleons live in the African rainforests. They can use their amazing eyes to look in two directions at once!

Frilled lizard
Found in the dry bushlands of Australia, this lizard puts up its frill to frighten off enemies.

River animals

World of Nature

All kinds of animal live in or near the world's rivers. Strong swimmers live in fast-flowing rivers, but most animals choose quieter streams.

Flying visitors

Bats swoop over the river at night to catch small flying insects.

Kingfishers catch fish by diving head first into rivers.

Herons stand in the water waiting to stab fish and eels with their sharp beaks.

Water rat
Water rats make their homes in the riverbank.

Beaver
Beavers build dams across small rivers. They use trees they have felled with their sharp teeth.

A beaver's home is called a lodge.

Mayfly
Mayfly young are called larvae and live underwater. The adults fly in the air above.

The lodge is built with logs above the water level.

Did you know?
Water beetles breathe underwater by trapping an air bubble under their wings.

Water snake
Water snakes have thick, scaly skins to keep out water.

River

Dam

Leeches
Leeches cling to stones on the river-bed, so they won't be swept away.

River shellfish
These shellfish live in fast-flowing water. They feed on water plants.

Trout
Trout live in swift, shallow streams. The females lay their eggs in the river-bed.

Crayfish
Crayfish live in fast-flowing rivers, feeding on small fish and worms.

Find out more ▷ Animal homes 16   Rivers and lakes 119

Rivers and lakes

Rivers are always on the move.
They carry rainwater downhill,
from mountains to the sea.

Did you know?
Some rivers contain water only once or twice a year when there is rain.

2 Stream
From the source, a small stream flows downhill. The water is clean and fast flowing.

A river's course
Rivers start life as a swift trickle, but as they flow into each other, they become slower and larger.

1 River source
Rainwater trickles into the ground and comes out at one place. This is a river's source.

—Shallow stream

—Fast-flowing water

—Big rocks

—Clear, clean water

3 River
The stream becomes a river as more water flows in. It forms big bends called meanders.

4 River mouth
The river flows into the sea. This is a river's mouth.

Uses of rivers and lakes

Water sports, such as fishing and sailing, are popular activities.

Hydro-electric power stations make electricity from the power of the river.

Water transport is an important way of moving goods from place to place.

Irrigation pumps water from lakes and rivers to dry fields, to help crops grow.

Lakes
Lakes are dips in the ground that are filled by rain and river water. Some lakes are built by people.

Reservoirs are built by people.

Crater lakes form naturally when rain collects inside a volcano.

Find out more ▷ River animals 118   Water 146

Science and Technology

Rocks and minerals

Minerals

Rocks are made of tiny grains called minerals. Some minerals form beautiful stones.

Opals are valued for their beauty.

Diamonds are the hardest of all minerals.

Jade is very hard. It is often used for carving.

Gold is a precious metal. It, too, is formed by minerals.

Copper pipe

Copper is an ore mineral. Most useful metals come from ore minerals.

Pencil

Graphite is one of the softest minerals. It is used in pencils.

The world around us is made of rock. We use rocks and minerals for many things, from buildings to jewellery.

Rock types

There are three main types of rock. They are formed in different ways.

Sedimentary rock

Sedimentary rock is made from layers of mud, sand, and stones that have been squashed together.

Conglomerate rock

Metamorphic rock

Metamorphic rocks are sedimentary or igneous rocks that have been changed by great heat, great pressure, or both.

Marble

Did you know?

The largest diamond in the world is called the Cullinand. It is as heavy as a pineapple.

Granite

Igneous rock

Igneous rock is made from hot, runny rock deep inside the Earth that has cooled and hardened.

Using rocks and minerals

Chalk is a soft sedimentary rock used for writing.

Chalkboards are made from metamorphic rock called slate.

Paint can be made from coloured minerals in rocks.

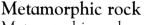

Azurite blue paint

Vermilion paint

Sculptures are often cut from igneous rocks, such as marble.

Tin cans used to be made from tin ore.

Find out more ▷ Earth 50   Early humans 49

Life in the Past

Romans

Roman life

Baths were places to relax and wash. They were built in every town.

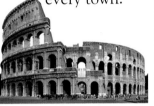

Amphitheatres were huge stadiums. Many public sports were played here.

Temples were fine stone buildings that the Romans built to worship their gods.

Fountains provided townspeople with fresh drinking water.

The Romans were a powerful people, who lived in Europe about 2,000 years ago. They ruled over a huge empire.

Roman soldier
The Roman army was one of the best in the world. Its soldiers were expertly trained and well armed.

Javelin

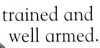

Armour of metal strips

Roman road
The Romans were great builders. Their roads were strong and very straight.

Backpack
A soldier carried a bag, tool kit, and pots and pans.

Woollen tunic

Weapons
In battle, soldiers fought with spears, swords, and daggers.

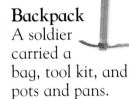

Sandals
A soldier's sandals were studded with nails so they'd last.

Belt
Every soldier wore a belt of leather and metal.

Shield

Emperor
For over 400 years, the Romans were ruled by emperors.

Coins stamped with emperor's portrait

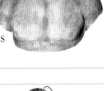

Emperors wore a crown of leaves.

Augustus

Did you know?
Roman men wore robes called togas. Trousers were thought to be unmanly!

Science

Types of scientist

Chemists produce new foods, drugs, and materials.

Radiologists take X-rays and study the results.

Forensic scientists study the clues that can solve crimes.

Zoologists study animals and how they live.

Geologists study rocks to find out about the Earth.

Science is observing, examining, and learning about the world around us. Scientists often find new ways to improve people's lives.

Laboratory
Many scientists work in laboratories. These rooms have the special equipment scientists need to perform and record experiment results.

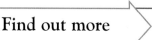

Bunsen burner

Chemical solutions

Scientist

Test tubes

Flask

Microscope

Did you know?
Isaac Newton worked out the laws of gravity when an apple fell on his head.

Experimenting
Scientists learn by doing experiments.

1 Scientists ask a question and say what they think the answer is.

2 They do tests to prove they are right.

3 They take measurements and make careful records as proof.

World of Nature

Sea animals

Salty seawater covers nearly three-quarters of the Earth's surface. Below the waves, the oceans teem with a huge variety of sea life.

Did you know?
Flying fish can leap from the water, spread out their fins, and glide through the air.

Starfish
Starfish cling to the rocky seashores of the Atlantic Ocean. They use their arms to pry open seashells.

Narwhal
The narwhal whale has a twisted tusk and lives in the icy waters of the Arctic Ocean.

Thornback ray
The flat thornback ray hides on the Pacific sea bed. It is well camouflaged against the sand.

Deep-sea hatchet
Named after its big, axe-like belly, this hatchet lives in the deep waters of the Pacific Ocean.

ARCTIC OCEAN

NORTH AMERICA

EUROPE

ASIA

PACIFIC

ATLANTIC OCEAN

AFRICA

SOUTH AMERICA

INDIAN OCEAN

OCEAN

AUSTRALASIA

ANTARCTICA

Dugong
Dugongs are gentle mammals that swim in large herds in the shallow waters of the Pacific.

Zooplankton
Billions of tiny sea creatures called zooplankton float in all the world's oceans.

Octopus
This octopus inhabits the warm coastal waters of the Atlantic. It wraps its prey up in its tentacles.

Sea horse
Sea horses are the only fish that swim upright. They are found among the coral reefs off Africa.

Sperm whale
Huge sperm whales eat tonnes of plankton a day. They live in the Atlantic and Pacific oceans.

Find out more Fish 67   Seas and oceans 124

World of Nature

Seas and oceans

Did you know?
The Marianas Trench is 11 km (7 miles) deep. It is the deepest part of the ocean.

From space, the Earth looks blue because most of it is covered by water. Below the waves is a secret world we are only just beginning to explore.

The **Arctic Ocean** is the smallest ocean. It freezes over in the winter months, and only icebreaker ships can get through.

Sea exploration

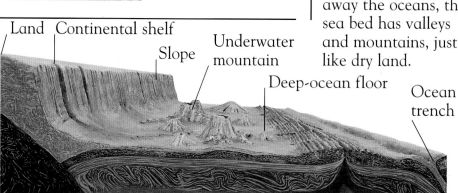

Canoes were used by the first explorers. They were carried by the wind and the sea.

Spanish sailing ship

The world's oceans
There are four main oceans in the world. They cover nearly three-quarters of the Earth's surface.

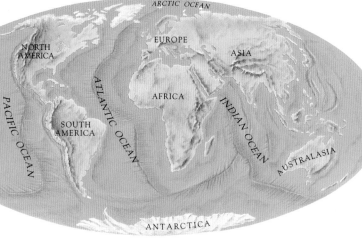

ARCTIC OCEAN

NORTH AMERICA

EUROPE

ASIA

ATLANTIC OCEAN

AFRICA

PACIFIC OCEAN

SOUTH AMERICA

INDIAN OCEAN

AUSTRALASIA

ANTARCTICA

Sailing ships were used by explorers 500 years ago to sail around the world.

Submarines are used by today's explorers to study the sea bed under the ocean.

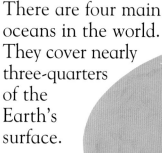

The **Pacific Ocean** is bigger than all the other oceans put together. It has huge waves.

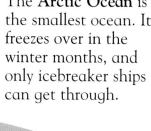

The **Indian Ocean** stretches between Africa and Australia. Coral reefs grow in the warm, shallow waters close to shore.

The sea bed
If you could drain away the oceans, the sea bed has valleys and mountains, just like dry land.

The **Atlantic Ocean** separates America from Europe and Africa. Huge container ships carry cargo between the continents.

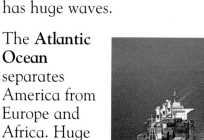

Land Continental shelf

Slope

Underwater mountain

Deep-ocean floor

Ocean trench

Find out more   Fish of the world 68   Ships and boats 127

World of Nature

Seashore

Did you know?
This crab holds a sea anemone in each of its pincers. If a fish attacks, the sea anemone stings it!

The seashore, where the sea meets the land, is home to a huge variety of plants and animals. They have all had to adapt to saltwater, strong winds, and waves.

Seashore life

Pipefish have very long, thin bodies and hide in seaweed.

Crabs hide in holes in rocks and wave their pincer claws at their enemies.

Seaweed   Snakelocks anemones   Winkle   Limpet

Snakelocks anemones use their stinging tentacles to kill their prey.

Crab

Rock pool
When the tide goes out, water is trapped in rock pools. Here, animals and plants can stay safely underwater.

Sea-urchin

Sponge

Starfish

Prawn

Seagulls eat almost anything, even dead fish on the beach.

Seaweed
Seaweeds are plants that grip rocks with sticky pads. Their leaves are called fronds.

Shells
Shells of all shapes and sizes can be found on the seashore. Each shell was once home to a sea creature.

The **goldsinny** is a tiny fish that lives only in rock pools.

Find out more Australasia 26   Seas and oceans 124

Seasons

In many parts of the world there are different seasons in the year. The changes they bring affect most living things.

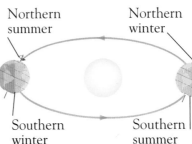

Northern summer

Northern winter

Southern winter

Southern summer

Earth and the seasons
We have seasons because the Earth tilts as it circles the Sun. When the north pole leans towards the Sun it is summer in the north and winter in the south.

Four seasons
In many parts of the world, there are four seasons in the year.

Spring
The weather warms up. Plants begin to grow and many animals are born.

Trees grow new leaves.

Lambs are born.

Summer
The days are long and warm. Flowers bloom and fruits grow.

Butterflies feed on flowers.

Plants flower.

Trees are in full leaf.

Winter
Winter days are dark and cold. Little grows in the frozen soil.

Some trees have no leaves.

Some animals hibernate all winter.

It may often snow.

Autumn
Autumn days are shorter and cooler. Nuts and berries ripen in the woods.

Some trees start to lose their leaves.

Squirrels collect nuts for winter food.

Did you know?
The Arctic tern spends summer at the north pole, then flies to the south pole for summer there!

Polar seasons
There are two seasons at the poles.

In summer, it is always light.

In winter, it is always dark.

Tropical seasons
There are two seasons in tropical areas – one wet and one dry.

For half the year, winds blow in from the sea, bringing heavy rains.

Find out more Climates 39   Earth 50

Ships and boats

Anchor
Anchors act as brakes. They dig into the seabed and stop ships moving.

Cruise ship
All boats do a particular kind of job. A cruise ship gives passengers a holiday at sea.

Ships and boats carry passengers and goods up and down rivers, over lakes, and from port to port across oceans and seas.

Rope
Rope is used a lot on boats. Special knots hold things in place.

Portholes are cabin windows.

Lifeboat

The bridge is where the captain controls the ship.

Anchor

Swimming pool

Rudder for steering

Hull

Types of boat

Hovercraft float on a cushion of air. Fans blow air downwards and lift the boat up.

Cargo ships carry huge containers full of heavy goods around the world.

Trawlers are fishing boats. They drag a net that scoops up fish from the sea.

Frigates have missiles onboard to strike enemy ships in times of war.

Did you know?
Cargo ships carry up to 2,700 containers. These would stand almost twice as high as Mount Everest.

Safety
All ships carry rescue equipment in case of accidents at sea.

Flares are like fireworks. They lead rescuers to where you are.

Life-jackets help people float if they fall into the water.

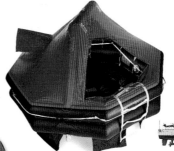

Life-rafts are used to carry passengers if their boat sinks.

Moving in water
Different boats move in different ways.

Motor boats have an engine that turns a propeller.

Rowing boats have oars to move them through the water.

Sailing boats are driven by the wind.

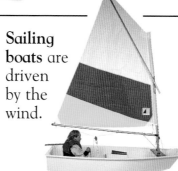

Paddle steamers go up and down rivers. They are driven by a wheel at the back.

Find out more ▷ Explorers 61   Transport 142

Skeletons

A set of bones, an outer case, a beautiful shell – almost all animals have some sort of skeleton. Skeletons support the body and protect the soft parts inside.

Animal skeletons

Tortoises have an inner skeleton joined to their exoskeleton, or shell.

Elephant skull
The long tusks are actually teeth!

Long, light bones help the cat run faster.

Human skull
The large skull encloses a big brain.

Hips

Skull

Snakes can curl up because they have hundreds of bones in their spine.

Long, pointed teeth to kill prey

Long tail for balance

Spine is long and bendy.

Rib cage protects heart and lungs.

Sharp claws to catch prey

Cat skeleton
Without a skeleton, most animals, like this cat, would be floppy bags of skin with no shape!

Fish have long, bendy spines to help them move through water.

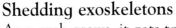

Exoskeleton
Many animals have a hard case or shell on the outside of their body. It is called an exoskeleton.

Beetle

Stiff plates make a hard casing that protects the beetle's soft body.

Shells
Some shells get bigger as the animal grows.

Shedding exoskeletons
As a crab grows, it gets too big for its shell. So the crab wriggles out of its old shell, and grows a new, larger one.

Did you know?
Worms have no bones at all. They are filled with fluid, which gives them their shape.

Birds have hollow bones, which make them light enough to fly in the air.

Frogs have short spines, but long back legs that are good for jumping.

Find out more ▸ Fossils 74   Human body : skeleton 82

Sound

The world is full of sounds. Some are useful, others are just annoying! But we hear them all in the same way.

Did you know?
Some singers can sing a note so high and so loud that it will shatter a glass!

Sound waves move outwards through the air.

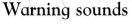

Skin vibrates, or shakes.

Sound waves
All sounds are made by vibrations that move the air and send out invisible sound waves to our ears.

Drum stick

Drum base

Warning sounds
Smoke detectors bleep loudly if a fire starts.

Alarm clocks ring to wake you in the morning.

Noise levels
The loudness of a sound is measured in decibels.

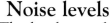

Falling leaves are quiet. Their noise measures 20 decibels.

Talking to people measures 30 to 60 decibels.

Vacuum cleaners reach 60 to 80 decibels.

Jumbo jets are very loud, making 140 decibels of noise!

Speed of sound

Light travels faster than sound. That is why you see lightning before you hear thunder.

Sound travels further in water than in air. Whales can hear up to 60 miles (100 km) away.

Musical sounds
Musical instruments make sounds in different ways.

Recorders make sounds when air vibrates inside the hollow tube.

A **double bass** makes sounds as its strings vibrate.

Find out more Music 100   Television 138

129

Continents of the World

South America

Central America and Caribbean
Central America's volcanoes, forests, and Caribbean sun-drenched islands are home to some exotic wildlife.

Volcano
On many of the islands, old volcanoes are covered by lush tropical rainforest.

Pitch lake
This lake in Trinidad is full of pitch – a black sticky tar on the ground.

Scarlet ibis
The ibis lives on the Caribbean islands. It pulls worms out of the mud with its long beak.

NASSAU

BAHAMAS

HAVANA

CUBA

Greater Antilles

Waterfall
The tropical islands have heavy rainfall. There are many spectacular waterfalls.

DOMINICAN REPUBLIC

HAITI

PORT-AU-PRINCE   SANTO DOMINGO

Virgin Islands   British Virgin Islands

SAN JUAN   Puerto Rico

Antigua & Barbuda

BELIZE
• BELMOPAN

JAMAICA
KINGSTON

Lesser Antilles

Guadeloupe

Dominica

Coral reef
Coral reefs in warm Caribbean waters are home to sponges and tropical fish.

GUATEMALA
GUATEMALA CITY •

HONDURAS
• TEGUCIGALPA

SAN SALVADOR •
EL SALVADOR

NICARAGUA
• MANAGUA

Bee hummingbird
Cuba is home to the world's smallest bird. Bee hummingbirds are the same size as a butterfly!

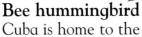
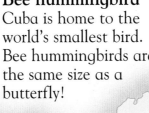

N

Martinique

ST LUCIA
BARBADOS

St Vincent and the Grenadines

Netherlands Antilles

Aruba

GRENADA

COSTA RICA
• SAN JOSÉ

PORT OF SPAIN   TRINIDAD & TOBAGO

Passion flower
Passion flowers grow in climbing vines in the forests.

PANAMA
• PANAMA CITY

Beach
White, sandy beaches stretch their way around the shoreline. They are fringed with coconut palms.

Mangrove tree
These trees grow in wet, boggy land along the many tropical coastlines.

Did you know?
• The Caribbean has some of the most dangerous storms in the world, called hurricanes.
• Hummingbirds are the only birds in the world that can fly backwards!

Find out more  Climates 39 Mountains 99

South America

South America

South America is home to the world's largest rainforest. It is bursting with colour and is a refuge for rare plants and animals.

Did you know?
- The Amazon rainforest is more than 12 times the size of France.
- Lake Titicaca is the highest lake in the world.

Howler monkey
The screams of howler monkeys echo through the forest.

River Amazon
The Amazon and it's surrounding rivers make up 20% of the world's freshwater.

Angel Falls
Angel Falls in Venezuela is the highest waterfall in the world.

Lake Titicaca
South America's largest lake lies high up in the Andes.

Atacama Desert
This desert in Chile is the driest place on Earth. Few living things can survive here.

Rainforest
Rainforests are being cut down to make way for roads and industry.

Andean condor
This eagle is the world's heaviest bird of prey!

The Andes
The Andes are the longest chain of mountains in the world.

Pampas
The Pampas are the dry, rolling grasslands in Argentina. They are used for cattle grazing.

Find out more ➤ Birds of the world 31 — Mountains 99

Continents of the World

South America: culture

Carnival, Brazil
Traditional festivals are still important today. Colourful dancers sway to modern music in this Brazilian carnival.

Brasilia
This cathedral lies in Brasilia, Brazil's capital city, which was built only 30 years ago.

The people of Central and South America enjoy both modern and traditional lifestyles. There is a great variety of culture and customs.

Elaborate headdress

Brightly coloured costume

Music
Music is very important to all South American cultures.

Steel drum

Guiro

Christ the Redeemer
This statue stands high above Rio de Janeiro in Brazil.

Culture

Arts and crafts, such as jewellery making, still follow traditional methods.

Cricket is the most popular sport on the Caribbean Islands.

Food, like Italian pasta, has been introduced from other countries.

Ancient ruins of long-ago cities lie hidden in the forests of Central America.

Industry

Oil has made Venezuela the richest country in South America.

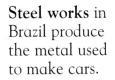

Copper mines in Chile are some of the largest in the world.

Steel works in Brazil produce the metal used to make cars.

Tourism is an important industry in South America. Many people flock to the beaches here.

Space travel

People have always wanted to know about space. For years scientists could only look up into the sky. Today, they can send up rockets to investigate.

Working in space
Astronauts leave the shuttle to do experiments.

Life in space

People float around in space because there is no gravity to hold them down.

Space shuttle
Astronauts inside the space shuttle are blasted into space on the back of a rocket.

Shuttle

Main fuel tank

Extra fuel tanks for take-off

USA

NASA
Atlantis

Space suits are special protective clothing. They help astronauts breathe in space.

Space orbit
Out in space, the rocket drops away from the shuttle, which then slowly orbits, or circles, the Earth.

Rocket fuel burning

Landing
On its return from space, the shuttle flies through the Earth's atmosphere and lands just like an ordinary plane.

Space food is different from normal food – it is dried to make it last.

SPACE FOOD

Did you know?
The *Saturn V* rocket had the most powerful engine ever. It used 3 tonnes (3.3 tons) of fuel per second!

Viewing space

Satellite dishes
on Earth collect information and pictures from satellites.

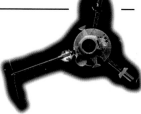

Satellites orbit in space. They send information back to Earth.

Space probes are sent into space to explore other planets.

Find out more ▷　　Communications 41　　　　Moon 98

World of Nature

Spiders and minibeasts

A spider in a corner, a snail in a wall, a worm underground – spiders and minibeasts live all around us, but keep well hidden.

Web spider
A spider is not an insect. Insects have six legs. Spiders have eight.

The silk comes out of the spinnerets

Webs
Web spiders make strong, sticky silk, which they spin into round orb webs to trap flying insects.

Two fangs grab prey.

Spiderlings
Baby spiders, called spiderlings, fly through the air on long pieces of silk.

This spider has eight eyes.

Each leg has six joints.

Abdomen

Minibeasts

Centipedes can move fast. They feed on insects and slugs.

Millipedes have up to 400 legs. Most feed on rotting plants.

Woodlice live where it's damp and shady. They feed on leaves.

Earthworms tunnel through soil, feeding on dead plants.

Scorpions kill their prey with the deadly sting on their tails.

Snails crawl along on their foot. They like to eat vegetables.

Did you know?
The pill millipede curls into a tight, solid ball when it's attacked by an enemy, such as a beetle or ant.

Hunting spiders
Not all spiders spin webs. Some hunt for food instead.

Chilean red-leg spiders eat mice and birds.

Trapdoor spiders ambush their unsuspecting prey.

Raft spiders can walk over ponds to find food.

Crab spiders kill insects with a poisonous bite.

Find out more ➤ Butterflies and moths 36   Insects 86

Life Today

Sport

Most people enjoy sport for the exercise and fun. But some people train hard to compete against the best athletes in the world.

Did you know?
Some skiers improve their technique by practising on top of fast-moving cars!

Olympic Games
The Olympics are the world's greatest sporting competition. They are held every four years.

Olympic medals
There are three medal winners in each event.

Running track

Olympic athletics stadium

Sporting competitions
The US Open is one of golf's great championships.

The **Cricket World Cup** is a competition between many nations.

The **Rugby World Cup** is a huge international tournament.

The **Formula 1 World Championship** is won by the fastest overall driver.

Paralympics
The Paralympics is an international competition for disabled athletes.

Sports rules
A referee or umpire makes sure players obey the rules. A blow on a whistle can stop the game.

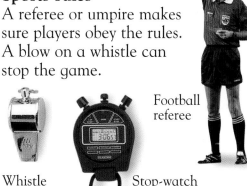

Football referee

Whistle   Stop-watch

Winter Olympics
The Winter Olympics is a competition of winter sports, such as skiing and ice skating.

Sports kit
Each sport has a special outfit, often in team colours. Other pieces of kit protect players from injury.

Baseball glove

Netball bib

Cricket pads

Ice-hockey helmet

US football shirt

The **Grand Slam** is four great tournaments in the tennis world.

Find out more   Human body: skin 83   Sports of the world 136

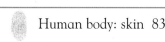

Life Today

Sports of the world

Ice hockey

Baseball

All over the world, sportsmen and women train hard to compete among the best in their chosen sport.

Did you know?
The world's heaviest Sumo wrestler weighs as much as four teenage boys.

Team sports
Most team sports are fast-moving ball games. The players in a team must work together to win.

Basketball

Attacker
Defender

Football

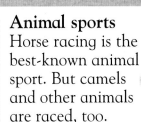

Skiing

Individual sports
In some sports, people compete alone, trying to score points, or racing against the clock.

One-to-one sports
In one-to-one sports, the players compete against one other person at a time.

Fencing

Animal sports
Horse racing is the best-known animal sport. But camels and other animals are raced, too.

Camel racing

Gymnastics

Squash

Horse racing

High jump

Water sports
Water sports take place on rivers, in the sea, or in swimming pools indoors.

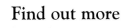
Surfing

Scuba diving

Swimming

Canoeing

Find out more

North America: culture 105   Romans 121

Science and Technology

Sun and stars

Studying stars

Astronomers use different instruments to view the stars.

Telescopes are the simplest way to look at the stars.

Observatories contain huge telescopes that can see many miles into space.

Space satellites send back pictures of stars to Earth.

Huge groups of stars in space are called galaxies. The galaxy we live in is called the Milky Way. Our Sun is just one of millions of stars in the Milky Way.

Sun

Like all stars, the Sun, is a huge ball of super-hot gas. It burns very brightly, giving Earth the heat and light it needs to support life.

Dark patches are called sunspots.

Eclipse

As the moon passes in front of the Sun, it blocks out most of its light. This is called an eclipse.

Did you know?

It would take about 20 years for a jumbo jet to travel from Earth to the Sun!

Solar-powered car

Solar power

The Sun's rays can be used to make electricity.

The hottest part of the Sun is it's centre. This is called the core.

The Sun's rays are so powerful, they can damage the human eye.

Mapping stars

On a clear night you can see thousands of stars in the sky. Astronomers have made maps of the stars.

Star map of the northern skies

Constellations

Groups of stars are called constellations. Each group is given a name.

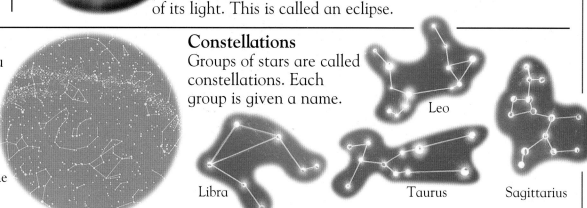

Leo

Libra

Taurus

Sagittarius

Find out more Light 90 Planets 109

Television

Television (TV) uses sound and moving pictures to broadcast sport, films, programmes, and news from around the world.

Did you know?
The smallest television in the world is so tiny it can fit on a wrist watch!

Television camera

Control room
People in the control room keep in close touch with the studio.

TV programmes

Cinema films are shown on television.

News programmes give daily reports and stories.

Television studio
Most TV programmes are made inside with special lights and cameras. The large rooms used are called studios.

On location
Some programmes are made outside using smaller, lighter, hand-held cameras.

Documentaries, such as wildlife films, are programmes about the real world.

Scenery

Lights Cameras

Presenter

Musical events can be watched by a huge audience all over the world.

Children's television is made to entertain and inform children.

How television works

1 Transmitters send out television signals as radio waves.

3 The television set turns the signals into sounds and pictures.

2 An aerial on the roof picks up the radio waves and sends signals to your television.

Satellite television
Some television signals are broadcast from satellites in space.

Satellite dish on roof

Find out more Electricity at home 53 Film 66

Life Today

Theatre

Types of play

A **tragedy** is a serious play, with a sad ending.

Operas are plays performed by singers to music.

Mime is the art of acting a story without saying a word.

Comedies are funny plays, intended to make people laugh.

For thousands of years, people have enjoyed going to the theatre to watch actors make a story come alive on stage.

Open-air theatre
In some countries, theatres are built in the open air.

Theatre building
The audience sit in rows on several different levels. The actors perform on a stage.

Downstairs is called the stalls.

Spotlight

Upstairs is called the circle.

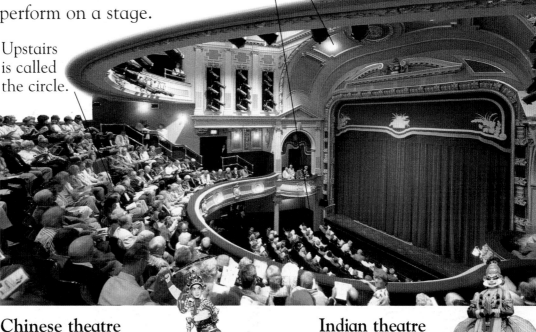

Chinese theatre
In China, the costumes actors wear tell the audience about their characters.

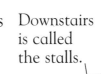

Indian theatre
Traditional Indian plays tell stories. The actors mime, sing, and dance.

Did you know?
The first theatres were built in Greece about 2,500 years ago.

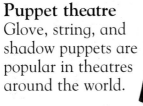

Puppet theatre
Glove, string, and shadow puppets are popular in theatres around the world.

Judy   Punch

Crocodile

Glove puppets, like Punch and Judy, are popular in Britain.

Shadow puppets are used in southeast Asia.

Marionettes have up to 20 strings to move them.

Life Today

Towns and cities

City services

Office buildings are where many people work.

Hospitals can be big enough to treat thousands of patients.

Shopping is easy in a city. There are lots of big stores.

Schools are dotted around a city for children of all ages.

Did you know?
The city of Venice, in Italy, is built on 108 islands. It has canals instead of roads!

Towns and cities are bustling places where thousands, or even millions of people live and work together.

City centre
City centres are often built around a central square, where there are many historical buildings.

Skyscrapers
Tall skyscrapers save space on the ground, and make an exciting skyline.

Fountains

Old buildings

City transport

Cable cars run on tracks and carry passengers up hills in some cities.

Buses are quick and easy for people travelling through the city streets.

Taxis are more expensive but are useful for people who are in a hurry.

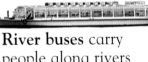

River buses carry people along rivers and stop at many landing points.

City entertainment
Cities have interesting places for people to visit or relax.

Parks are quiet, green spaces, away from the busy streets.

Cafés are places to eat, drink, and watch the people passing by.

Museums and galleries have interesting objects and paintings to view.

Find out more   Africa: culture 8    Homes and houses 78

Trains

Types of train

Breakdown trains clear fallen trees and broken trains off the tracks.

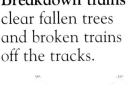

Crocodile trains pull carriages up steep mountains. They can "bend" round corners.

Shunters are mighty engines that push and pull other trains in a train yard.

Goods trains transport heavy loads such as coal and oil across the country.

From the puffing steam train of the past to the electric "bullets" of today, trains provide high-speed transport for both passengers and goods.

Electric train

Most modern, high-speed passenger trains get their power from an electric cable above the track.

Driver's cab

Electric cable

Lights

Diesel train

These trains are powered by engines that run on diesel oil.

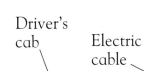

Smoke from burning coal

Signal

In early days, simple signals made the railways safer.

Steam train

The first trains used the power of steam to drive the engine.

Bell   Whistle

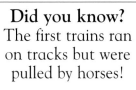

City trains

Underground trains carry passengers under the busy city streets.

Electric track

Monorails run on a single track high above the busy roads.

Magnetic levitation (maglev) trains float above a track. Strong magnets push the train into the air!

Find out more ▷ Electricity 52   Magnets 93

Transport

Life Today

Transport of the world

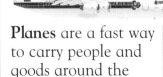

Planes are a fast way to carry people and goods around the world.

Tuk-tuks are small trucks used as taxis in Thailand.

Bicycles are cheap and clean. They are popular in China.

Paddle steamers carry people up and down rivers.

Trams are electric buses, running on rails in some city centres.

People use all kinds of transport to travel long or short distances, and to carry heavy loads from place to place.

Different vehicles

Although new forms of transport are being invented all the time, some traditional vehicles are still in use.

A modern bullet train from Japan

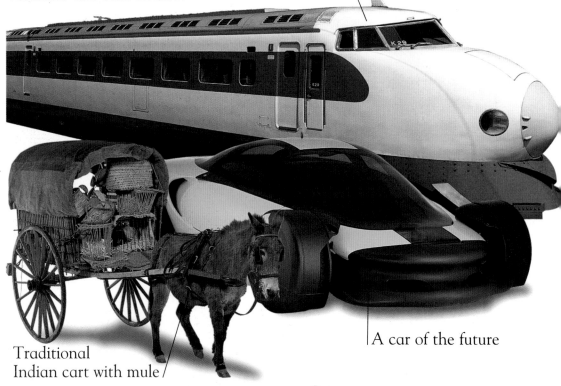

Traditional Indian cart with mule

A car of the future

Animal transport

Elephants in Asia carry very heavy loads The driver is called a mahout.

Donkeys are very strong. They can carry people up steep mountain paths.

Camels are often called ships of the desert. They can carry goods and people in the heat.

Find out more Aircraft 10   Bicycles 29

World of Nature

Trees

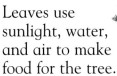

Because of their size, it's easy to forget that trees are plants. But like any plant, they have roots, a stem, leaves, and flowers that make seeds.

Did you know?
The world's tallest tree is a coast redwood in North America. At 111 m (151 ft) it is taller than the Statue of Liberty in New York.

Oak tree
Every part of this deciduous oak tree helps it to survive and grow.

Leaves
Leaves use sunlight, water, and air to make food for the tree.

Leaves will fall off in the autumn.

Branches, twigs, and leaves make up the crown of the tree.

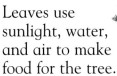

Trunk
The trunk is the strong stem that sucks up food and water from the soil.

Trunk

Acorns
Acorns are the seeds of the oak tree.

Roots grow under the ground

Bark
The bark protects the trunk.

Tree products
Paper is made from mashed up wood.

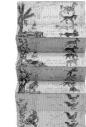

Sculptures, such as totem poles, may be carved out of a whole tree trunk.

Maple syrup is made from the sweet juice of the sugar maple tree.

Furniture is made of wood from the trunks and branches of trees.

Unusual trees

Bonsai trees are dwarf trees, which are grown in pots.

Palm trees grow on sandy beaches.

Baobab trees survive in the desert by storing water in their trunks.

Mangrove trees grow in swamps. Their roots arch out over the water.

Find out more ➤ Forests 73   Rainforest animals 113

Science and Technology

Trucks

Types of truck

Tankers carry liquid goods, such as oil, petrol, or milk, around the country.

Road sweepers collect rubbish from the streets and keep our towns tidy.

Removal vans carry the furniture when people are moving house.

Car transporters carry new cars from the factory to the showroom.

Snowploughs have a large shovel at the front to clear snow from the roads.

Articulated truck

This truck has two main parts – the cab at the front and the trailer at the back.

Engine under driver's cab

Huge trucks rumble along our roads both night and day. Most carry goods around the country, but some are used for emergencies.

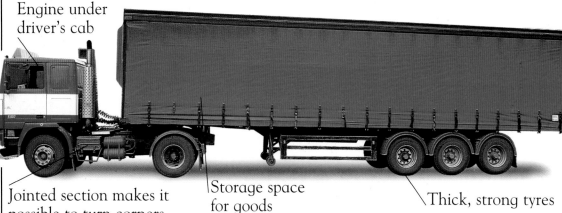

Jointed section makes it possible to turn corners.

Storage space for goods

Thick, strong tyres

Exhaust
Diesel fumes from the engine come out through the exhaust stack.

Inside a cab
Many large trucks have a bed in the cab so the driver can rest on long journeys.

Wheels
Trucks have lots of wheels to support their heavy loads.

Did you know?
The very first trucks were steam powered. Coal was shovelled into a boiler as the truck moved along!

Emergency trucks

Ambulances take people who are ill or hurt to hospital.

Tow-away trucks take vehicles to a garage for repairs.

Fire engines carry fire-fighters, water pumps, and hoses to the scene of a fire.

Find out more Building machines 34   Factories 62

Life Today

Vikings

The Vikings from Scandinavia lived over 1,000 years ago. They sailed all over Europe and west to America fighting, trading, and settling.

Invading warrior
A Viking warrior attacked villagers on the coast.

Metalwork

Bronze items, like this key, were often highly decorated.

Silver jewellery, like this brooch, was worn by wealthy people.

Viking ships
The Vikings sailed great distances in strong, fast boats called longships.

Prowhead
The prowhead was a carving at the front of the ship.

Mast

Sail made of wool or linen

Single square sail

Room for 80 warriors

Steering oar
This oar was used to steer the boat.

Snake-tail ornament

Prowhead

Steering oar

Iron shears were used to cut cloth and shear sheep for their wool.

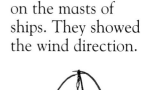

Rowing oar

Weather vanes sat on the masts of ships. They showed the wind direction.

Did you know?
Some Viking warriors prepared for battle by working themselves into a frenzy and going berserk. They were called berserkers!

Trade
The Vikings travelled far and wide, exchanging goods for gold and silver.

German glass cup

Coins

Scales to weigh goods

Weights for scales

Cooking pots made from iron or soapstone were hung over a fire.

Science and Technology

Water

Dissolving
Some things seem to disappear when mixed with water. This is called dissolving.

Dirt dissolves in water. That is why you wash!

Minerals in rocks can dissolve in water. They sometimes form stalactites in caves.

Oxygen dissolves in water. Fish need this oxygen to live.

Salts in rock dissolve in water. They make seawater salty.

Water is the most important liquid on Earth. It has no smell, colour, or taste but without it people couldn't survive.

Water cycle
Water is always moving from the sea, to the sky, to the land. This is called the water cycle.

3 River
The rain runs into rivers, which flow to the sea.

Fast flowing stream

4 Sea
The river empties its water into the sea, and the cycle starts all over again.

Ice
Ice is so powerful, it can cut huge valleys into hard rock.

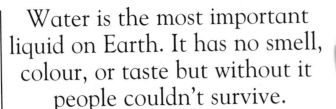

1 Evaporation
The Sun's heat turns water into water vapour. This rises, cools, and forms clouds.

2 Rain
Winds blow the clouds over the land. Water in the clouds falls as rain, snow, or hail.

Water for life
Every living thing needs water to survive.

Did you know?
The Dead Sea in Israel is so salty that people can sit up and float in it without sinking!

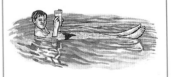

Forms of water
Water can change its form. It can be solid ice, a runny liquid, or steam – a gas that mixes with air.

Solid   Liquid   Gas

Find out more ➤ Living things 91   Seas and oceans 124

Weather

Wind, sun, rain, or snow – weather is what happens in the air around us. Weather affects our lives, so forecasts warn us when it will change.

Recording the weather

Anemometers spin round quickly. They measure the speed of the wind.

Weather buoys gather information about all kinds of weather condition.

Thermometers measure how hot or cold the air is.

Barometers are used to measure the pressure of air.

World weather
Satellites in space take pictures of the Earth. This one shows patterns of cloud around the world.

Storm clouds

Rain clouds over the Equator

Europe is sunny.

Clear skies over northern Africa

Did you know?
The biggest hailstone in the world fell in North America. It was as heavy as 13 tennis balls.

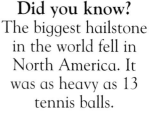

Tornado
These strong, whirling winds twist at up to 500 km/h (300 mph).

Snow
Rain turns to snow when the air is very cold.

Fog
Fog is a type of cloud that forms low down on the ground.

Rain

1 Clouds are made of tiny water droplets that float in the air.

2 The clouds get darker as more water droplets join together.

3 The droplets grow bigger and heavier until they fall to the ground as rain.

Find out more ▸   Air 9   Seasons 126

World map

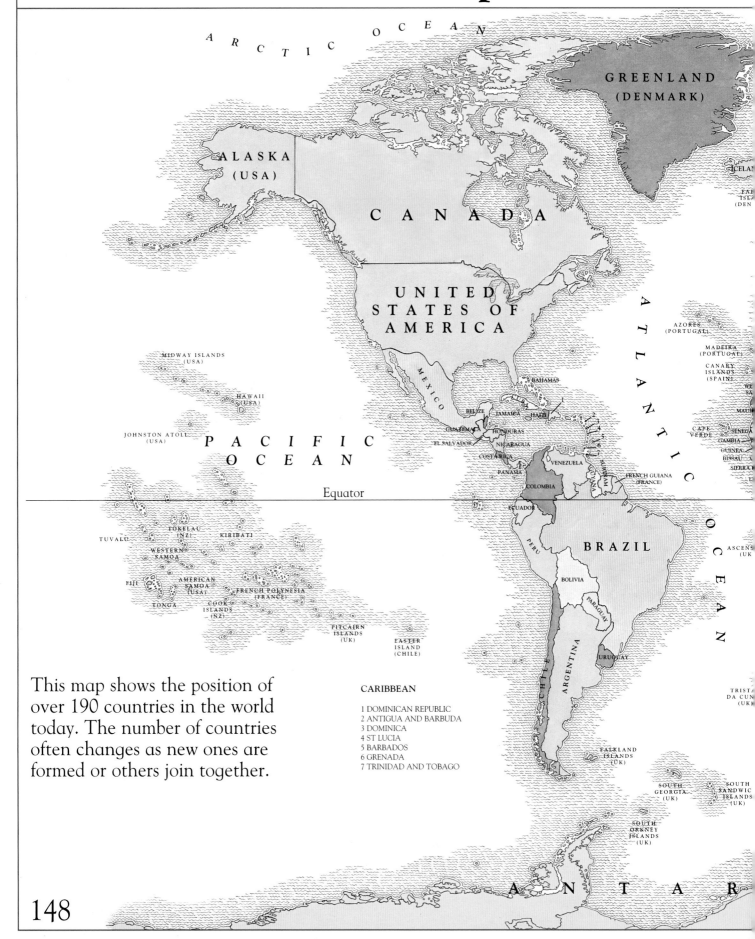

ARCTIC OCEAN

GREENLAND
(DENMARK)

ALASKA
(USA)

ICELAN

FAE
ISL
(DEN

CANADA

ATLANTIC

UNITED
STATES OF
AMERICA

AZORES
(PORTUGAL)

MADEIRA
(PORTUGAL)

MIDWAY ISLANDS
(USA)

MEXICO

BAHAMAS

CANARY
ISLANDS
(SPAIN)

WE
SA

HAWAII
(USA)

BELIZE

JAMAICA

HAITI

MAUI

JOHNSTON ATOLL
(USA)

GUATEMALA
HONDURAS

CAPE
VERDE

SENEGA

PACIFIC
OCEAN

EL SALVADOR
NICARAGUA

GAMBIA

GUINEA-
BISSAU

COSTA RICA

VENEZUELA

SIERRA

PANAMA

FRENCH GUIANA
(FRANCE)

Equator

COLOMBIA

ECUADOR

OCEAN

TUVALU

TOKELAU
(NZ)

KIRIBATI

PERU

BRAZIL

ASCENS
(UK

WESTERN
SAMOA

BOLIVIA

FIJI

AMERICAN
SAMOA
(USA)

FRENCH POLYNESIA
(FRANCE)

PARAGUAY

TONGA

COOK
ISLANDS
(NZ)

PITCAIRN
ISLANDS
(UK)

EASTER
ISLAND
(CHILE)

ARGENTINA

URUGUAY

TRISTA
DA CUN
(UK

This map shows the position of
over 190 countries in the world
today. The number of countries
often changes as new ones are
formed or others join together.

CARIBBEAN

1 DOMINICAN REPUBLIC
2 ANTIGUA AND BARBUDA
3 DOMINICA
4 ST LUCIA
5 BARBADOS
6 GRENADA
7 TRINIDAD AND TOBAGO

FALKLAND
ISLANDS
(UK)

SOUTH
GEORGIA
(UK)

SOUTH
SANDWIC
ISLANDS
(UK)

SOUTH
ORKNEY
ISLANDS
(UK)

ANTAR

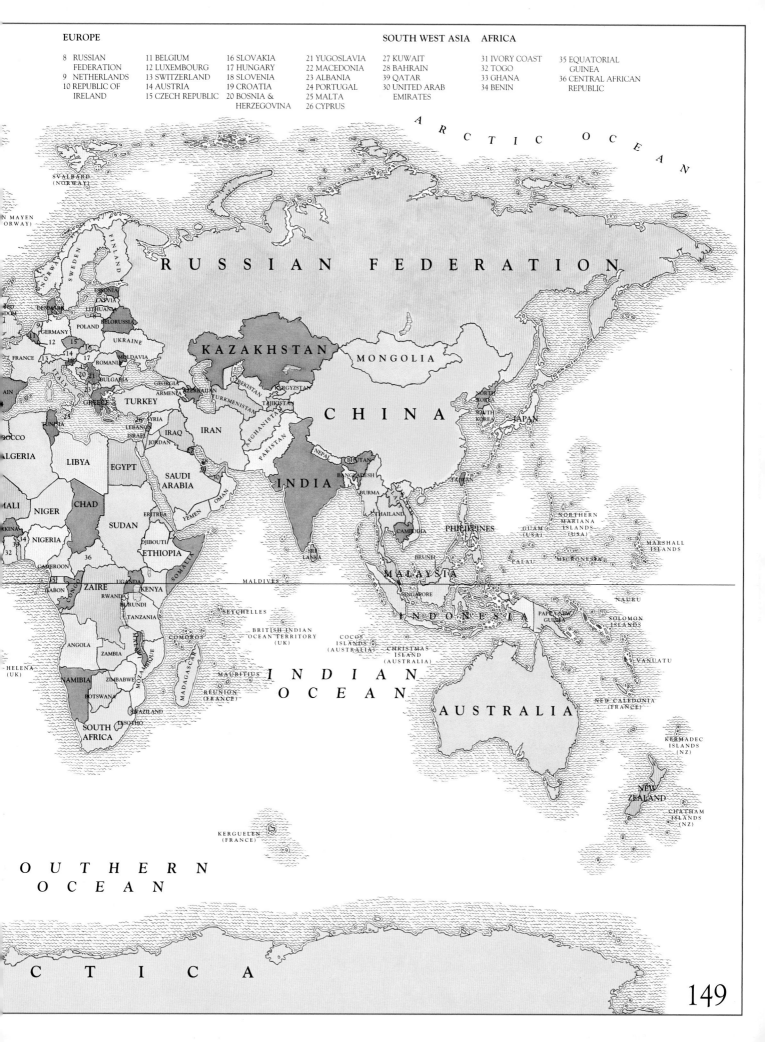

EUROPE

8	RUSSIAN FEDERATION	11 BELGIUM	16 SLOVAKIA	21 YUGOSLAVIA
9	NETHERLANDS	12 LUXEMBOURG	17 HUNGARY	22 MACEDONIA
10	REPUBLIC OF IRELAND	13 SWITZERLAND	18 SLOVENIA	23 ALBANIA
		14 AUSTRIA	19 CROATIA	24 PORTUGAL
		15 CZECH REPUBLIC	20 BOSNIA & HERZEGOVINA	25 MALTA
				26 CYPRUS

SOUTH WEST ASIA

27 KUWAIT
28 BAHRAIN
39 QATAR
30 UNITED ARAB EMIRATES

AFRICA

31 IVORY COAST
32 TOGO
33 GHANA
34 BENIN
35 EQUATORIAL GUINEA
36 CENTRAL AFRICAN REPUBLIC

ARCTIC OCEAN

SVALBARD (NORWAY)

N MAYEN (NORWAY)

RUSSIAN FEDERATION

NORWAY
SWEDEN
FINLAND
ESTONIA
LATVIA
LITHUANIA
DENMARK
BELORUSSIA
GERMANY
POLAND
UKRAINE
MOLDAVIA
ROMANIA
BULGARIA
GEORGIA
ARMENIA
AZERBAIJAN
GREECE
TURKEY
FRANCE
ITALY
SPAIN

KAZAKHSTAN
MONGOLIA
UZBEKISTAN
KIRGYZSTAN
TURKMENISTAN
TAJIKISTAN

CHINA

SYRIA
LEBANON
ISRAEL
IRAQ
JORDAN
IRAN
AFGHANISTAN
PAKISTAN

NEPAL
BHUTAN
BANGLADESH
INDIA
BURMA

NORTH KOREA
SOUTH KOREA
JAPAN

TAIWAN

TUNISIA
MOROCCO
ALGERIA
LIBYA
EGYPT
SAUDI ARABIA
MALI
NIGER
CHAD
SUDAN
ERITREA
YEMEN
OMAN
BURKINA
NIGERIA
CAMEROON
ETHIOPIA
DJIBOUTI
SOMALIA

THAILAND
CAMBODIA
PHILIPPINES
BRUNEI
SRI LANKA
MALDIVES

GUAM (USA)
NORTHERN MARIANA ISLANDS (USA)
MARSHALL ISLANDS
PALAU
MICRONESIA

CONGO
GABON
ZAIRE
UGANDA
KENYA
RWANDA
BURUNDI
TANZANIA
ANGOLA
ZAMBIA
MALAWI
COMOROS
SEYCHELLES

MALAYSIA
SINGAPORE
INDONESIA

PAPUA NEW GUINEA
NAURU
SOLOMON ISLANDS

BRITISH INDIAN OCEAN TERRITORY (UK)
COCOS ISLANDS (AUSTRALIA)
CHRISTMAS ISLAND (AUSTRALIA)

VANUATU

NAMIBIA
BOTSWANA
ZIMBABWE
MOZAMBIQUE
MADAGASCAR
MAURITIUS
RÉUNION (FRANCE)

INDIAN OCEAN

NEW CALEDONIA (FRANCE)

HELENA (UK)

SWAZILAND
LESOTHO
SOUTH AFRICA

AUSTRALIA

KERMADEC ISLANDS (NZ)

KERGUELEN (FRANCE)

NEW ZEALAND

CHATHAM ISLANDS (NZ)

OUTHERN OCEAN

CTICA

World map: continents

This world map shows all seven continents. Each continent, except for Antarctica, is made up of several countries.

North pole

South pole

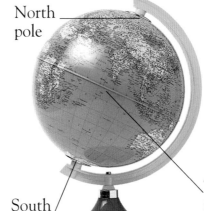

Globe
A globe is a round map of the world. The Earth spins around an invisible pole, called the north pole, at the top and the south pole at the bottom.

North America
North America stretches from the North pole almost to the Equator.

Europe
This is one of the smallest continents, but has one of the largest populations.

Asia
Asia is the biggest continent and has the largest population.

The Equator is an imaginary line that divides the Earth in half.

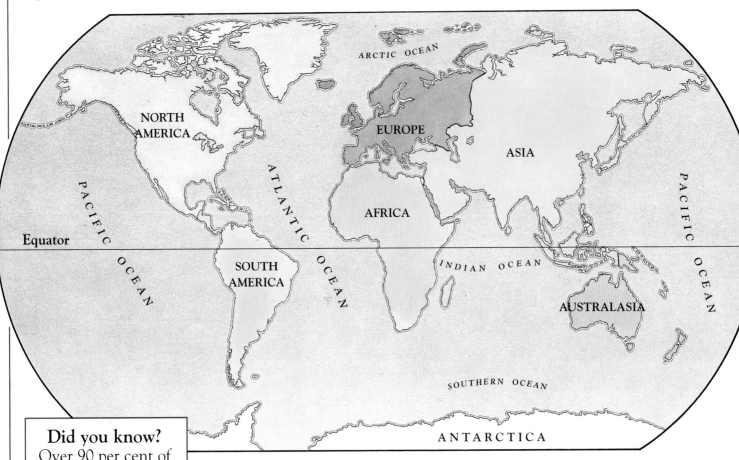

ARCTIC OCEAN

NORTH AMERICA

EUROPE

ASIA

PACIFIC OCEAN

ATLANTIC OCEAN

AFRICA

PACIFIC OCEAN

Equator

SOUTH AMERICA

INDIAN OCEAN

AUSTRALASIA

PACIFIC OCEAN

SOUTHERN OCEAN

ANTARCTICA

Did you know?
Over 90 per cent of the world's ice can be found in the continent of Antarctica.

South America
South America stretches all the way from the Equator almost to the south pole.

Africa
Africa is the second largest continent. The Equator runs through the centre of it.

Australasia
This area includes Australia, which is the smallest continent, and many other small islands.

Antarctica
This is the coldest and most southerly continent. No one lives here permanently.

United Kingdom

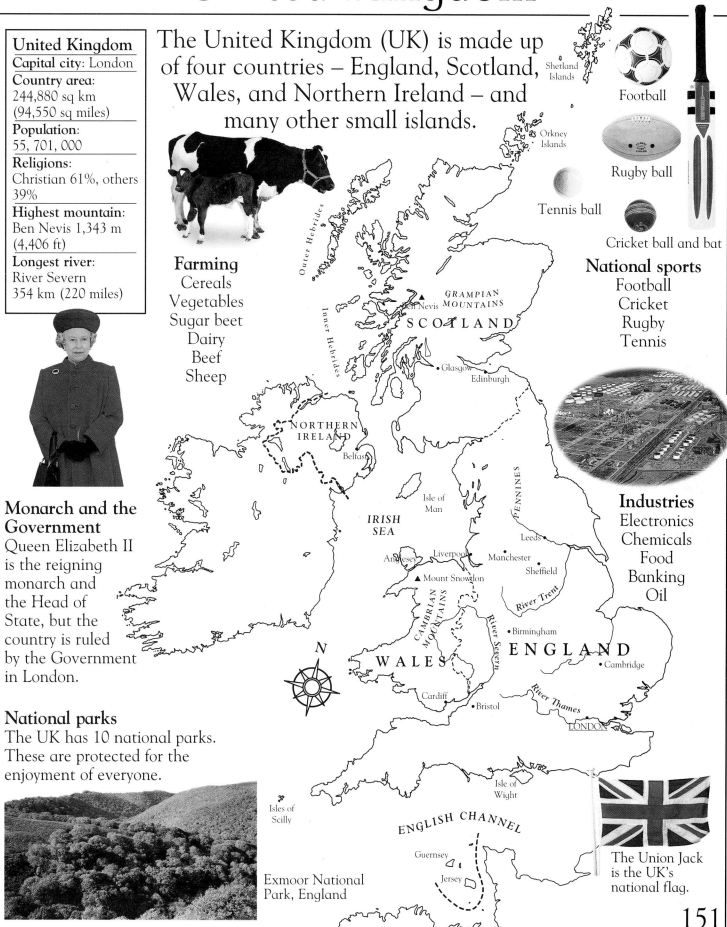

United Kingdom
Capital city: London
Country area:
244,880 sq km
(94,550 sq miles)
Population:
55, 701, 000
Religions:
Christian 61%, others
39%
Highest mountain:
Ben Nevis 1,343 m
(4,406 ft)
Longest river:
River Severn
354 km (220 miles)

The United Kingdom (UK) is made up of four countries – England, Scotland, Wales, and Northern Ireland – and many other small islands.

Football

Rugby ball

Tennis ball

Cricket ball and bat

National sports
Football
Cricket
Rugby
Tennis

Farming
Cereals
Vegetables
Sugar beet
Dairy
Beef
Sheep

Monarch and the Government
Queen Elizabeth II is the reigning monarch and the Head of State, but the country is ruled by the Government in London.

National parks
The UK has 10 national parks. These are protected for the enjoyment of everyone.

Exmoor National Park, England

Industries
Electronics
Chemicals
Food
Banking
Oil

Shetland Islands

Orkney Islands

Outer Hebrides

Inner Hebrides

GRAMPIAN MOUNTAINS

Ben Nevis

SCOTLAND

• Glasgow

Edinburgh

NORTHERN IRELAND

Belfast

Isle of Man

PENNINES

IRISH SEA

Leeds •

Liverpool

Anglesey

Manchester •

Sheffield •

▲ Mount Snowdon

River Trent

CAMBRIAN MOUNTAINS

River Severn

• Birmingham

ENGLAND

WALES

• Cambridge

Cardiff •

• Bristol

River Thames

LONDON

N

Isle of Wight

Isles of Scilly

ENGLISH CHANNEL

Guernsey

Jersey

The Union Jack is the UK's national flag.

151

World history timeline

This timeline lists some of the important events in world history and shows when they happened.

Early people begin to make tools from stones.

BC 30,000

Flint arrow-head

Hieroglyphs **Ancient Egypt** is at the height of its power.

3,000

BC means before the birth of Christ.

AD means after the birth of Christ.

Jesus Christ is crucified about this time.

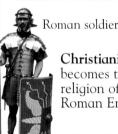
Emperor Augustus

The **Roman Empire** grows across Europe.

Roman soldier

Christianity becomes the official religion of the Roman Empire.

Mayan statue

Mayan civilization develops in Central America.

| AD 1 | 30 | 100 | 391 | 600 |

The **plague** kills one-third of Europe's population.

The **Aztec and Inca empires** grow in Central and South America.

Statue of a llama

The **first printed book** in Europe – the Bible – is made in Germany.

The **Renaissance** brings great changes to life in Europe. It is a time of learning in science and art.

Painting by Leonardo da Vinci

| 1347–1351 | 1350–1519 | 1455 | 1450–1600 |

The **English Civil War** ends and King Charles I is executed.

The execution of Charles I

Peter the Great becomes ruler of Russia. He improves industry and education.

The **American War of Independence** ends British rule in the USA.

George Washington becomes the first president of the USA.

| 1649 | 1682 | 1775–1783 | 1789 |

Canada becomes independent from Britain.

The first **motor car** is invented by the German Karl Benz.

1898 Benz "Velo"

English hunting in India

The **British Empire** is at its peak.

Australia gains independence from Britain.

The first successful **aeroplane flight** is made by American Orville Wright.

| 1867 | 1885 | 1804–1885 | 1901 | 1903 |

Australia welcomes about 2 million settlers from Europe.

Gandhi leads the movement for Indian independence from Britain.

Mao Tse-tung makes China a communist republic.

Germany is split into West Germany and communist East Germany.

Mount Everest, the world's high mountain, is climbed by Edmund Hillary and Sherpa Tenzing Norgay

| 1945 | 1947 | 1949 | 1953 |

Judaism spreads throughout western Asia.

Star of David

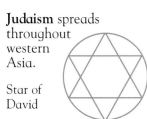

2,000

Ancient Greek civilization is at its peak. The Parthenon is built in Athens.

Greek vase

500

Buddhism starts in India with the birth of its founder, Siddhartha Gautama.

563

The **Chinese Empire** begins when Shih Juang-ti unites China, and becomes its first emperor.

Shih Juang-ti

221

The prophet **Muhammed** begins the religion of Islam.

622

Vikings from Scandinavia travel widely to find new lands and trading partners.

Viking longship

800

Christian Crusaders from Europe fight to re-gain control of Jerusalem from the Muslims.

Crusaders

1096–1291

Italian-born **Christopher Columbus** crosses the Atlantic Ocean.

Astrolabe

1492

The **world is round** and not flat. This was discovered by Spanish explorers.

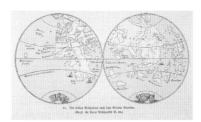

1500

Japan stops all contact with foreigners and the outside world for the next 200 years.

1639

The **slave trade** grows. Many Africans are seized and shipped to America.

1600–1800

The **French Revolution** brings down the monarchy in France.

1789

Steam trains are invented. They are powered by wood or coal.

1830

Maori rebellion in New Zealand ends British rule. New Zealand is allowed to govern itself.

1850

Civil War breaks out between the states of America. Slaves are set free.

1861

World War I is fought in Europe.

1914–1918

The **Russian Revolution** overthrows the Tzar. Lenin becomes the new communist leader.

Vladimir Illich Lenin

1917

The **Great Depression** is a time of great hardship in the USA.

1929

World War II breaks out after German leader Hitler invades Poland.

British fighter plane

1939–1945

The **Vietnam War** is fought. American troops help South Vietnam.

1965–1973

Neil Armstrong is the first person to walk on the moon.

1969

The **Berlin Wall** comes down as East and West Germany reunite.

1989

Nelson Mandela becomes President of South Africa.

1994

153

Index of entries

A

Aboriginals 26, 28
abstract paintings 107
Abu Dhabi 24
accidents, hospitals 79
acid rain 73
Afghanistan 24, 149
Africa 6–8, 100, 148–149, 150
air 9, 43, 73, 91
aircraft 10, 152
airports 10
airships 10
Alaska 102, 103, 148
Albania 59, 149
Algeria 6, 149
alligators 117
alphabets 32
Alps 56, 59
aluminium foil 97
Amazon River 131
ambulances 144
America see United States of
   America
American Civil War 153
American Samoa 148
American War of
   Independence 152
amphibians 11, 17
anchors 127
Andes 131
anemometers 147
Angel Falls 131
Angola 7, 149
animals 15, 16, 17, 18, 91
Antarctica 19, 112, 148–9, 150
Antigua & Barbuda 130, 148
Antilles, Greater 130
Antilles, Lesser 130
ants 72, 86, 113
apartment blocks 78
Arabs 61
Aral Sea 22
archers 38
Archimedes 92
Arctic 112
Arctic Ocean 124, 148
Ardennes 55
Argentina 131, 148
Armenia 22, 149
armour, knights 89
Armstrong, Neil 153
art 107
arteries 84
Ascension 148

Asia 20–5, 149, 150
asteroids 109
astronauts 98, 133
astronomers 137
Atacama Desert 131
Atlantic Ocean 124
Atlas Mountains 6
atmosphere 50
Augustus, Emperor 152
Australasia 26–8, 149, 150
Australia 26, 28, 149, 152
Austria 55, 149
autumn 126
Ayers Rock 26
Azerbaijan 22, 149
Azores 148
Aztecs 152

B

babies 80
badgers 72
Bahamas 130, 148
Baikal, Lake 22
ballet 44
balloons 10
bamboo 77
bananas 71
Bangladesh 24, 25, 149
baobab trees 7
Barbados 148
barometers 9, 147
Barosaurus 48
baseball 136
basketball 136
bats 15, 95, 118
batteries 52
bears 16, 72, 95, 102, 111
Beaufort scale, wind 9
beavers 118
Beethoven 100
beetles 86, 128
Belgium 55, 56, 149
Belize 130, 148
Belorussia 22, 23, 149
Benin 6, 149
Benz, Karl 152
Berlin Wall 153
Bhutan 24, 25, 149
Bible 32, 115, 152
bicycles 29, 92, 142
birds 17, 30–1, 72, 118
bison 55
Black Forest 55
Blackbeard 108

blind people, Braille 32, 81
blood 84
Blue Mountains 26
boats see ships and boats
Bolivia 131, 148
Bollywood 25
Bombay 25
bones 82, 128
books 32
Borneo 20
Bosnia and Herzegovina 59,
   149
Botswana 7, 149
Braille 32, 81
brain 84
Brasilia 132
brass instruments 101
Brazil 65, 131–2, 148
bricks 35
bridges 33
British Empire 152
broken bones 82
Bronze age 49
Brunei 20
Buddhism 21, 115, 153
buildings 34, 35, 38, 60
Bulgaria 59, 149
bulldozers 34
bungalows 78
Burkina 6, 149
Burma 20, 149
Burundi 7, 149
buses 140
bush-babies 95
butterflies 18, 36, 51, 86

C

Cabinda 7
cable cars 140
cacti 46, 110
cafés 140
calcium 82
calculators 42
calories 54
Camargue 59
Cambodia 20, 149
camels 45, 142
Cameroon 6, 149
Canada 102, 103, 148, 152
Canary Islands 148
candles 65, 90
canoes 124, 136
Cape Verde 148
caravans 78

carbohydrates 70
carbon dioxide 9
Caribbean 130, 132
carnival 132
Carpathian Mountains 55
cars 37, 62, 88, 142
cartoon films 66
Caspian Sea 22
castles 38
caterpillars 36
Catholic Church 60
catkins 69
cats 15, 128
cattle 63
cave paintings 49
CD Roms 32
centipedes 72, 134
Central African Republic 6,
   149
Central America 130, 132, 148
Central Europe 55–6
cereals 64, 77
Chad 6, 8, 149
Chad, Lake 6
chalk 120
chameleons 117
Charles I, King of England 152
châteaux 60
Chatham Islands 149
cheetahs 76
chemical energy 54
chemistry 122
chickens 63, 91
Chile 131, 132, 148
China 20, 149
   Ancient China 12, 153
   Chinese New Year 65
   theatre 139
   trade 61
chocolate 62, 71
Christianity 65, 115, 152
Christmas 65
cities 8, 140
climates 39
clothing, early humans 49
clouds 147
clownfish 16
coal 52, 54
cobras 117
Colombia 131, 148
colour 40
Columbus, Christopher 61, 153
combine harvesters 64
communications 41, 88
Comoros 149

compact discs 88
compasses 12, 93, 96
Compsognathus 47
computer games 88
computers 41, 42, 53
Congo 7, 149
coniferous forests 73
conservation 43
constellations, stars 137
continents 150
Cook, Mount 27
Cook Islands 148
copper 120
coral reefs 130
Corsica 59
Corythosaurus 47
Cossacks 23
Costa Rica 130, 148
Cotswolds 57
cotton 97
cowboys 103
crabs 16, 125, 128
crafts 8, 23, 25, 105, 132
cranes 34
crater lakes 119
craters, moon 98
Cretaceous period 48
cricket 135
Croatia 59, 149
crocodiles 18, 116
cruise ships 127
Crusaders 153
crustaceans 17
Cuba 130, 148
Cyprus 149
Czech Republic 55, 56, 149

D

damselflies 86
dance 8, 44, 65
Danube, River 55
Dead Sea 146
Death Valley 104
deciduous forests 73
Deinonychus 47
demolition balls 34
Denmark 57, 58, 149
desert animals 45
deserts 39, 46
diamonds 120
diesel trains 141
digestion 70
dingos 76
dinosaurs 47–8, 74
Djibouti 6
doctors 79
dogfish 51
dolphins 95

Dominica 148
Dominican Republic 130, 148
donkeys 142
dragons 12
drums 129

E

eagles 30, 31
early humans 49
Earth 50
    magnetic poles 93
    as a planet 109
    seasons 126
earthquake detectors 12
earthworms 72, 134
eastern Asia 20–1
eating 70
echidnas 76
eclipse, Sun 137
Ecuador 131, 132, 148
Edison, Thomas 88
Edmontonia 47
education, Ancient Greece 14
eels 68
eggs 11, 51, 67
Egypt 6, 149
    Ancient Egypt 13, 152
Eiger, Mount 55
El Salvador 130, 148
electric light 90
electric trains 141
electrical energy 54
electricity 52–3, 88
electronic instruments 101
elephants 128, 142
embryo 80
emperors:
    Ancient China 12, 153
    Roman Empire 121
energy 43, 52, 54
England 57
English Civil War 152
entertainment 88
Equator 148–149, 150
Equatorial Guinea 7, 149
Eritrea 6, 149
Estonia 57, 149
Ethiopia 6, 149
Etna, Mount 59
Euoplocephalus 47
Europe 55–60, 61,
    149, 150
evaporation 146
Everest, Mount 24, 152
Everglades 104
exoskeleton 128
experiments, science 122
explorers 61

F

factories 62
Falkland Islands 148
families, animal 15
farming 8, 28, 63, 103, 105
Faeroe Islands 148
fax machines 41
feathers 30
fencing 136
festivals 65
fiction 32
Fiji 27, 28, 148
film 66
finches 30
fingerprints 83
Finland 57, 149
fire 49
fire engines 144
fireworks 90
fish 17, 67–8
    families 15
    farming 63
    river fish 118
    sea fish 123
    skeletons 128
fishing 58, 60, 71, 103
fjords 27, 57
flamenco dancing 44
flies 86
flowers 69, 114
flying 10, 30, 152
foetus 80
fog 147
food 64, 70–1
football 136
forensic scientists 122
forests 72, 73, 103, 114
fossils 48, 74
France 59, 60, 149
French Guiana 131, 148
French Polynesia 148
French Revolution 153
frigates 127
frogs 11, 51, 128
fruit 64, 75, 114
Fuji, Mount 20
furniture 143

G

Gabon 7, 149
galaxies 137
Gambia 6, 148
Gandhi 152
Ganges, River 24
gas 9, 52, 54
gears 92
geckos 113

geologists 122
Georgia 22, 149
Germany 55, 56, 149, 152, 153
geysers 27, 57
Ghana 6, 149
Gibraltar 59
glaciers 102, 112
glass 97
gliders 10
globe 150
glow-worms 90
goats 95
Gobi Desert 20
God 115
gods, Ancient Greece 14
gold 120
golf 135
Grand Canyon 104, 105
graphite 120
grasses 69, 77, 110
grasshoppers 86
grassland animals 76
grasslands 77
Great Barrier Reef 26
Great Britain *see* United
    Kingdom
Great Depression 153
Great Lakes 102, 104
Great Rift Valley 7
Great Wall of China 12
Greece 59, 149
    Ancient Greece 14, 153
    culture 60
    festivals 65
    houses 78
    theatre 139
Greenland 102, 148
Grenada 148
growth, human body 80
Guadeloupe 130
Guam 149
Guatemala 130, 148
Guinea 6, 149
Guinea-Bissau 6, 148
guinea pigs 76
Guyana 131, 148
gymnastics 136

H

hail 147
hair 83
Haiti 130, 148
Halloween 65
hamsters 76
Hawaii 148
hearing 81
heart 84
heat energy 54

helicopters 10
helmets 89
hieroglyphs 13, 152
high jump 136
Hillary, Edmund 152
Hindus 115
history timeline 152–3
Hitler 153
Hoggar Mountains 6
Hollywood 105
Holy Week 65
homes and houses 53, 78
Honduras 130, 148
horses 89, 136
hospitals 79, 140
hot-air balloons 10
houseboats 78
houses 35, 78
hovercraft 9, 127
human body 80–4
humans, early 49
hummingbirds 30, 130
Hungary 55, 149
hydro-electric power 52, 119

I
ice 146
ice hockey 136
icebergs 19, 112
icefields 112
Iceland 57, 148
igneous rock 120
Iguanodon 47–48
Incas 85, 152
India 24, 25, 100, 139, 149
Indian Ocean 124, 149
Indonesia 20, 149
industry 21, 23, 103, 105, 132
insects 17, 86-7
  spiders and minibeasts 134
Internet 41
inventions 88
invertebrates 17
Iran 24, 149
Iraq 24, 149
Ireland 57, 148
Iron age 49
irrigation 119
Islam 115, 153
Israel 24, 25, 149
Italy 59, 60, 149
Ivory Coast 6, 149

J
jade 120
jaguars 113
Jainism 115

Jamaica 130, 148
Jan Mayen 148
Japan 21, 149, 153
Java 20
Jerusalem 153
Jesus Christ 65, 115, 152
joints 82
Jordan 24, 149
Judaism 115, 153
Jupiter 109
Jurassic period 48
jute 25

K
kangaroos 94
Kashmir 24
Kazakhstan 22, 149
Kenya 7, 149
Kerguelen 149
Kilimanjaro, Mount 7
kimonos 21
Kiribati 148
kitchens 53
kites 12
kiwis 27
knights 89
koala bears 26
Koran 115
Krak des Chevaliers 38
Kremlin, Moscow 23
krill 111
Kuwait 24, 25, 149
Kyrgyzstan 22, 23, 149

L
laboratories 122
ladybirds 86
lakes 68, 119
landscapes 107
Laos 20, 149
Lapland 58
Latvia 57, 149
leather 62
leaves, trees 73, 143
Lebanon 24, 149
Lenin 153
Leonardo da Vinci 152
leopards 94
Lesotho 7, 149
letters 41
levers 92
Liberia 6, 149
libraries 32
Libya 6, 149
lichen 99
light 53, 90, 91
light energy 54

lighthouses 35
lighting 53
lightning 52, 90
lilies 69
lions 15
Lithuania 57, 149
living things 91
lizards 116, 117
llamas 63, 85
locusts 87
London 57, 58
Luxembourg 55, 149

M
Macedonia 59, 149
machines 34, 54, 64, 92
Machu Picchu 85
McKinley, Mount 102
Madagascar 7, 149
Madeira 148
magazines 41
Magellan 61
magnets 93
Malawi 7, 149
Malaysia 20, 21, 149
Maldives 149
Mali 6, 149
Malta 149
mammals 17, 94–5
Mandela, Nelson 153
mangrove swamps 20
Mao Tse-tung 152
Maoris 28, 153
maps 96
Mardi Gras 65
markets, Africa 8
marmosets 16
Mars 109
Marshall Islands 149
marsupials 94
Martinique 130
materials 97
Mauritania 6, 148
Mauritius 149
Mayan civilization 152
medicine 88
meerkats 15, 76
memory 84
Mercury 109
Meseta Plain 59
metamorphic rock 120
meteorites 109
Mexico 100, 104, 105, 148
mice 95
Micronesia 149
microwaves 53
Midsummer's Day 65
Midway Islands 148

migration 111
Milky Way 137
millipedes 72, 134
mime 139
minerals 8, 19, 70, 120
mining, Australia 28
Mississippi, River 104
Moldavia 59, 149
molluscs 17
Mongolia 20, 21, 149
monkeys 113
monorails 141
Monument Valley 104
moon 98, 153
Morocco 6, 100, 149
Moscow 23
mosses 110
moths 36, 86
motor racing 135
motorbikes 29
mountains 9, 99
Mozambique 7, 149
mudskippers 68
Muhammed 115, 153
mummies 13
murals 107
Muscat 24
muscles 82
museums 140
mushrooms 73
music 100
  Africa 8
  Asia 21
  festivals 65
  musical instruments 101
  sound 129
  South America 132
Muslims 115

N
Namib Desert 7
Namibia 7, 149
narwhals 123
Native Americans 41, 44, 103
Nauru 149
navigation 108
Nepal 24, 149
Neptune 109
nerves 84
nervous system 84
nests 51
Netherlands 55, 56, 149
New Caledonia 27, 149
New Guinea 78
New York 105
New Zealand 27, 28, 149, 153
newspapers 41
Newton, Isaac 122

newts 11
Niagara Falls 102
Nicaragua 130, 148
Niger 6, 149
Nigeria 6, 78, 149
Nile, River 6, 13
noise 129
nomads 25
non-fiction books 32
North America 102–5, 148, 150
North Korea 20, 149
north pole 112
northern Africa 6
northern Asia 22-3
northern Europe 57-8
Northern lights 93, 102
Northern Mariana Islands 149
Norway 57, 58, 149
nuclear power 52
nurses 79

O

oak trees 143
oasis 46
observatories 137
octopuses 17, 123
offices 35, 140
oil 25, 52, 54, 106
Okefenokee swamp 104
olive oil 71
Olympic Games 14, 135
Oman 24, 149
opals 120
opaque materials 90
operas 139
orang-utans 18
oranges 25
Orthodox churches 60
ostriches 30, 63
otters 95
outback 26, 77
ovens 53
Oviraptor 47
owls 31, 111
oxygen 9, 146
ozone layer 50

P

Pacific Islands 27, 148–149
Pacific Ocean 61, 124, 148
paddle steamers 127, 142
paint 40, 120
painting 49, 107
Pakistan 24, 149
Palau 149
pampas 77, 131

Panama 130, 148
pandas 18, 20
paper 12, 143
Papua New Guinea 26, 28, 149
papyrus 13
parachutes 9
paraffin oil 106
Paraguay 131, 148
Paralympics 135
parks 140
parrots 30
Parthenon 14
peaches 71
penguins 31, 111
percussion instruments 101
perfume 69
Peru 131, 148
petals 69
Peter the Great 152
petrol 106
pharaohs 13
Philippines 20, 149
pigs 63
Pinnacles, Australia 26
piranhas 68
pirates 108
Pitcairn Islands 148
pitchforks 64
plague 152
planes 10, 142
planets 109
plants 46, 91, 99, 110, 112
plastic 97
Plateosaurus 48
plays 139
ploughs 64
Pluto 109
Poland 55, 56, 149
polar lands 112
pollination 69
pollution 18, 43
polyester fabric 97
porcupines 95
portraits 107
Portugal 59, 60, 149
power stations 52
Prague 38, 55, 56
prairies 77
preserving food 70
proteins 70
Provence 59
Psittacosaurus 47
Puerto Rico 130, 148
pulleys 92
pulse 84
punishment, pirates 108
puppets 21, 139
pyramids 13

Q

Qatar 24, 149
Quebec 103

R

rabbits 16
raccoons 72
radiologists 122
radios 41
railways 141
rain 146, 147
rainbows 40
rainforests 6, 20, 26, 114, 131
animals 113
recycling 43, 97
Red Sea 24
reflection 90
reflex actions 84
refrigerators 53
reindeer 95, 111
religion 115
Renaissance 152
reptiles 17, 116–17
desert animals 45
dinosaurs 48
reservoirs 119
Reunion 149
rheas 15, 76
Rhine, River 55
rhinoceroses 95
rice 64, 71
Rio de Janeiro 132
rivers 68, 118, 119, 146
Riyadh 24, 25
robins 30
robots 42
rocks 120
Rocky Mountains 104
rodeos 103
Romania 59, 149
Romans 121, 152
Rome 59, 60
rope 127
rubber trees 21
rugby 58, 135
Russian Federation 22, 23, 149
Russian Revolution 153
Rwanda 7, 149

S

Sahara Desert 6
sailing boats 61, 127
St Helena 148
St Lucia 130, 148
salamanders 11
Sami people 58

Samurai warriors 89
sand, deserts 46
Sardinia 59
satellites 50, 133
maps 96
satellite dishes 88, 133
space 137
television 138
weather 147
Saturn 109
Saudi Arabia 24, 149
savanna 76, 77
scales 92
schools 140
science 122
scorpions 15, 134
Scotland 57, 58
scuba diving 136
sculptures 120, 143
scythes 64
sea horses 123
seagulls 125
seals 18, 111
seaplanes 10
seas and oceans 68, 123, 124, 146
seashore 125
seasons 126
seaweeds 110, 125
secretary birds 76
sedimentary rock 120
seeds 69, 73, 75, 110
Seismosaurus 47
Senegal 6, 148
senses 81
Serengeti Plain 7
servals 76
Seychelles 149
shadows 90
shanty towns 8
sharks 15, 68
sheep 27, 28, 63
shells 125, 128
Shih Juang-ti, Emperor 153
ships and boats 61, 108, 124, 127, 145
shops 140
shrubs 110
Siberia 22, 23
Sicily 59
sieges 38
Sierra Leone 6, 149
sight 81
sign language 41, 81
Singapore 20
skeletons 82, 128
skiing 136
skin 83
skulls 128

skyscrapers 35, 140
slave trade 153
slopes 92
sloths 113
Slovakia 55, 149
Slovenia 59, 149
slugs 51
smell, sense of 81
snails 134
snakelocks anemones 125
snakes 18, 113, 116, 117, 128
snow 147
Socrates 14
solar power 52, 137
Solar System 109
soldiers 89, 121
Solomon Islands 27, 149
Somalia 6, 149
Sonoran Desert 104
sound 54, 81, 129
South Africa 7, 149, 153
South America 130–2, 148, 150
South Georgia 148
South Korea 20, 149
south pole 19, 112
South Sandwich Islands 148
southern Africa 7
southern Asia 24–5
southern Europe 59–60
space probes 133
space shuttle 133
space travel 133
Spain 38, 44, 59, 85, 149
spiders 15, 134
sponges 97
sport 135–6
spring 126
squash 136
squirrels 16, 72
Sri Lanka 24, 25, 149
starfish 17, 123
stars 137
steam trains 141, 153
steel 97
Stegocerous 47
Stegosaurus 47
steppe 77
sticklebacks 68
streams 119
submarines 124
Sudan 6, 149
Sumatra 20
summer 126
Sumo wrestling 136
Sun 137
  climates 39
  energy 54
  light 40, 90

Solar System 109
surfing 136
Surinam 131, 148
Swaziland 7, 149
Sweden 57, 58, 149
swimming 136
Switzerland 55, 56, 78, 149
Sydney Opera House 28
Syria 24, 149

T

Table Mountain 7
tadpoles 11
Taiwan 20, 149
Taj Mahal, Agra 25
Tajikistan 22, 149
talking 41
Tanzania 7, 149
Tasmania 26, 149
taste 81
taxis 140
tea 25, 71
telephones 41, 53, 88
telescopes 137
television 41, 53, 88, 138
temples, Ancient Greece 14
tennis 135
Tenzing Norgay, Sherpa 152
tepees 78
termites 16
textiles, Africa 8
Thailand 20, 21, 149
Thanksgiving 65
thatch 35
theatre 14, 35, 139
thermometers 147
Tibet 20
tigers 18
tiles 35
tin cans 120
Titicaca, Lake 131
toads 11
Togo 6, 149
tools 49, 85
tornadoes 147
tortoises 116
touch 81
tourism 8, 19, 28, 60, 105
tournaments 89
tower blocks 78
towns 8, 140
tractors 64
trade, Vikings 145
trains 141, 142
trams 142
Trans-Siberian railway 23
translucent materials 90
transparent materials 90

transport 140, 142
travellers 61
trawlers 127
treasure 108
trees 73, 110, 143
Triassic period 48
Triceratops 47
Trinidad & Tobago 130, 148
Troodon 47
tropical seasons 126
trucks 144
tuk-tuks 142
tundra 22, 102, 112
Tunisia 6, 78, 149
tunnels 33
Turkey 24, 149
turkeys 63
Turkmenistan 22, 149
turtles 116, 117
Tuvalu 148
Tyrannosaurus rex 48

U

Uganda 7, 149
Ukraine 22, 149
Uluru 26
United Arab Emirates 24, 149
United Kingdom 57, 58, 149
United States of America 104, 105, 148
Ural mountains 22
Uranus 109
Uruguay 131, 148
Uzbekistan 149

V

Vanuatu 27, 149
Vatican City 60
vegetables 64, 71
veins 84
Venezuela 131, 132, 148
Venice 140
Venus 109
vertebrates 17
Victoria Falls 7
videophones 41
Vienna 55, 56
Vietnam 20, 149
Vietnam War 153
Vikings 61, 145, 153
villages 8, 21
virtual reality 42
vitamins 70
volcanoes 27, 99, 119, 130
Volga, River 22

W

wadis 24
wallabies 76
walruses 111
Wannanosaurus 48
Washington, George 152
wasps 51, 86
water 43, 70, 91, 146
water sports 136
weapons 38, 89, 108, 121
weather 39, 126, 147
webs, spiders 134
weevils 72
western Asia 24–5
Western Sahara 6, 148
Western Samoa 148
whales 94, 123
wheat 71
wheelbarrows 12
wheels 88, 92
wind 9, 52, 147
winter 126
Winter Olympics 135
wolves 72, 111
wood 35, 97
woodlice 134
woodwind 101
wool 63
World War I 153
World War II 153
worms 128
Wright, Orville 152
writing 41, 80
  alphabets 32
  hieroglyphs

X, Y, Z

X-rays 88
Yangtze River 20
Yemen 24, 149
Yugoslavia 59, 149
Zaire 7, 149
Zambezi, River 7
Zambia 7, 149
zebras 7, 95
Zimbabwe 7, 149
zoology 122
zooplankton 123
zoos 18

Acknowledgments

Additional editorial assistance Stella Love and Susan Peach

Additional design assistance Peter Radcliffe and Cheryl Telfer

Additional picture research Garifalia Boussiopoulou and Tom Worsley

Index Hilary Bird

Cartography Roger Bullen

Jacket design Sophia Tampakopoulos

Additional illustrations

Angelika Elsebach, John Hutchinson, Ruth Lindsay, Daniel J Pyne, Gill Tomblin, John Woodcock, Colin Woolf.

Photography

Peter Anderson, Sarah Ashen, Jane Burton, Paul Bricknell, Geoff Brightling, Peter Chadwick, Andy Crawford, Geoff Dann, Philip Dowell, Mike Dunning, Andreas Von Einsiedel, Neil Fletcher, Lynton Gardiner, Max Gibbs, Steve Gorton, Frank Greenway, Bob Guthany, Alan Hills, Michael Holford, Colin Keates, Gary Kevin, Barnabas Kindersley, Dave King, Bob Laneirish, C. Laubscher, Richard Leeny, Ruth Lindsay, Mike Linley, Andrew McRobb, Tony Morrison, David Murray, Martin Norris, Stephen Oliver, Roger Philips, Tim Ridley, Dave Rudkin, Saville Garden (Windsor), James Stephenson, Karl Shone, Steve Shott, James Stevenson, Clive Streeter, Harry Taylor, Kim Taylor, Peter Visscher, Barrie Watts, Matthew Ward, Steven Wooster, Jerry Young, Michael Zabe.

Picture agency credits

The publisher would like to thank the following for their kind permission to reproduce the photographs:
t=top, c=centre, b=bottom, r=right, l=left, a=above.

Ancient Art & Architecture: R. Sheridan 13bcr, J.P. Stevens 13bc.
Aerofilms: 121tr.
Allsport: S. Bruty 135c, P. Cole 135cl, C. Cole 135cr, M. Cooper 136bcr, M. Hewitt 135cr, A. Murrell 132, D. Pensinger 136crb, G.M. Prior 135crb, B. Radford 135cra, P. Roudean 135cr, R. Stewart 103cra, 136tr, cra, cr.
Ardea: G. Behrens 119cb, L. Bomford 15br, F. Gohier 45c, E. Haagner 15cra, C. Haanger 15cra, P. Morris 75bc, 67bc, P. Steyn 15crb, J. Swedberg 30tl / 15cr, br, 19br, 130ca, 130tr, 119bc, 118cla.
Barnaby's Picture Library: 34c / B. Gibbs 33c, 33clb.
BBC Natural History Unit: Phil Chapman 19ca.
Bildarchiv Foto Marburg: 89tc.
BMW GB Ltd: 57cb.
Bridgman Art Library: 115c, crb.

British Library: 32cla.
British Antartic Survey: 19bc.
Bruce Coleman: 15bc, 19cl, crb, 20clb, 24bc, 58tr, cb, cl, 60crb, 76cr, 96c, cr, 102c, 102crb, 104 cb, 110cb, 115c, 122bl, 130cla, cb, 146cr / E&P Bauer 111cr, J. Burton 134tc, J. Cancalosi 104c, E. Chrichton 24cla, G. Cubitt 21cla, 7tc, R. Forest 39cl, K. Gunnar 99br, T.O. Hounsen 60clb, J. Johnson 76c, H. Kranawetter 115cra, O. Langrand 105tc, A. Manzannres 15cb, Charlie Ott 112tr, Andy Prue 16bc, Hans Reinhard 20br, 27cl, 68cl, K. Rujhby 27cr, Kim Taylor 143br, U. Walz 119c, Konrad Wothe 143bc, J. Worrall 52clb, C. Zuber 75bl.
BT Corporate Pictures: 42cr.
Cadbury Ltd: 62c.
Central Broadcasting: 138c, tc, cra.
Collections: Patrich Wise 121cl.
Colorific: Steve Razzetti 24bc / 71br.
The Colour Museum, Bradford: 40bl.
Donald Cooper: 139c.
Corbis Bettman: 62tr.
Lupe Cunha: 79tr, c.
James Davis: 20cl.
Environmental Images: 23cb.
ET Archive: 121crb.
Eye Ubiquitous: 59bl / 147tl Chris Rose.
Fiat: 132bc.
Ronald Grant Archive: 66bl, crb, tr, cra.
Robert Harding: 7crb, tr, 9bc, 10tc, c, 19cla, 24bl, 25crb, tr, bl, 26tl, 28bc, tr, 32c, 39bl, 44cl, 55br, 56cr, 60cr, tr, 65cra, cb, 71bl, 78bc, cl, cra, 103br, 104ca, 105clb, cra, 115bl, bc, br, 130cl, 132cb, 140c, 148tr, cla, tl, bc / G. Hoberman 113c, cr, A. Tovy 12c, Dr T. Waltham 103cb.
Paul Harris: 102cb, crb.
Michael Holford: 38clb, 61cb.
Holiday Film Corp: 98cb.
Holt Studios: Nigel Cattlin 21clb.
House and Interiors: 106tl.
Hulton Getty: 19clb.
The Hutchison Library: 13tc, 23br, 44bl, 56cb, 85 br, cr, 93 cra, 103ca / N. Froggatt 56cra, ND Kenna 71cla, A. Tully 56bc.
ICCE: 7cla C. Aveling.
Image Bank: 6tr, 20cla, 24tl, clb, 28cra, 32bc, 33bc, 44br, 51cla, bl, 52crb, cb, c, 62ca, cra, cr, crb, br, bl, 65bcr, tr, 78cb, cr, 79cl, c, 90cr, 98br, 99bc, 100crb, cra, c, 114crb, 122cl, cla, tl, c, 124clb, bl, 126cra, cr, cb, 136bc, 138cra, bl, 142bc, 146cla, c / S. Allen 133bcr, A. Becker 59ca, PG Bowater 106cb, 63cr, D. Brownell 104tl, L. Gatz 41tr, Kay Churnogh 81tr, W. Clark 60crb, L. Castenada 140tl, David de Lossy 91bl; L. Dennis 58clb, W. Dietrech 38br, P. Doherty 88bl, 34bl, P. Eden 140cla, L. Gatz 41tr, J. Gocia 45c, Grant V. Faint 57br,